Build Financial Confidence and Change Your
Money Story—One 5-Minute Reset at a Time
(For ADHD Brains That Struggle with Finances)

THE

An ADHD Friendly System for Money Mastery

5 MINUTE
MONEY
RESET

SCOTT ALLAN

FROM THE CREATOR OF DO THE HARD THINGS FIRST®

The 5-Minute Money Reset

—for ADHD Brains—

Scott Allan

Also By Scott Allan

The 5-Minute Money Reset

ADHD-Friendly Financial Habits to Stop Overspending, Reduce Stress, and Reset Your Money in Just 5 Minutes a Day

Scott Allan

NEVER STRUGGLE WITH CONFIDENCE AGAIN—DOWNLOAD THE FEARLESS CONFIDENCE ACTION GUIDE AND BUILD LIMITLESS CONFIDENCE TODAY!

Click Here: <u>Download the Fearless Confidence Action Guide</u>

<u>scottallanbooks.com</u>

Contents

"If you don't know where your money is going, it's probably going somewhere you didn't want it to."

—Dave Ramsey

For You—A Message from the Author

I never intended to write a book about money and ADHD. For most of my life, I avoided talking about my financial struggles altogether. The shame ran too deep.

Everyone else seemed to have figured out the money game. I felt like I was perpetually struggling with rules that seemed obvious to everyone else.

On paper, things should have worked. I made decent money. I understood financial concepts. I even taught others about goal-setting and discipline. Yet my own financial life was constant chaos, avoidance, and shame.

I'd start budgeting systems with enormous enthusiasm. For two days, I'd track everything perfectly. By day three, I'd miss recording something.

By day four, I'd feel behind.

By day seven, I'd abandon everything, telling myself I'd "start fresh next month."

But next month never came. Instead, I'd avoid my accounts until something forced me to look—a declined card, an overdraft notice, or anxiety so painful I couldn't ignore it anymore.

It wasn't until my ADHD diagnosis in my mid-thirties that everything clicked. I wasn't lazy or irresponsible—I had a brain that processed financial information differently.

Standard advice to "make a budget and stick to it" wasn't failing because I lacked discipline. It failed because it wasn't built for how my brain worked.

That realization started my financial reset.

I stopped forcing myself into neurotypical systems. Instead, I built tiny habits that worked *with* my brain's need for novelty, immediate feedback, and emotional regulation. I called these micro-actions "resets"—ways to reconnect with money without overwhelming myself.

These small actions worked where elaborate systems had failed. I felt more connected to my finances. The anxiety faded. I caught problems earlier. Most importantly, I stopped disappearing when things got hard.

I wrote this book because I know what it's like to feel stuck in financial shame and avoidance. I know what it's like to have people tell you to "just be more responsible" when your brain physically struggles with the attention and emotional regulation that financial stability requires.

This isn't about becoming perfect with money. It's about becoming *present* with it.

If you've picked up this book, you're already taking a step toward reconnection. You're not broken. You're not behind. You're exactly where you need to be to begin again.

One reset at a time.

Scott Allan

https://scottallanbooks.com/

Introduction: This Isn't a Budget Book.

If you've ever opened your bank app and instantly felt your chest tighten—

If you've ever avoided a credit card statement because you couldn't handle seeing the number—

If you've ever told yourself, *"I'll get it together... next week"* (but didn't)—

This book is for you.

And if you live with ADHD—or struggle with ADHD-like symptoms like procrastination, impulsive spending, overwhelm, or emotional shutdowns around money— this book was **built** for you.

Because most financial systems aren't designed for the way your brain actually works.

They rely on:

- Long-term consistency

- Daily discipline

- Delayed gratification

- Linear thinking

- Emotional neutrality

That's exactly why they fall apart when you need them most.

You don't need more shame. You don't need more spreadsheets. You need a **reset**—one you can come back to over and over, even when things get messy.

Why This Book Exists

I didn't write this because I'm a financial expert who always had it together.

I wrote this because for years, I struggled with:

- Avoiding my finances when anxious

- Spending to soothe emotions, then hating myself for it

- Building systems I never followed through on

- Watching money slip away because I couldn't track it

- Believing deep down that I was "bad with money" and always would be

What changed wasn't some miracle budget. It was a series of tiny resets. Micro wins. One small action at a time—repeated until I believed I could show up again.

This book gives you that system. Not a quick fix. Not a complete overhaul. But a **repeatable, ADHD-friendly rhythm** that brings you back into your finances with clarity, courage, and compassion.

What's Inside

This is a short book on purpose.

Each chapter teaches you one idea, one tool, or one reset you can start using today—even if your brain feels tired, distracted, or stuck in shame.

Inside, you'll find:

- A reset ritual for when you avoid your bank account

- A 5-minute audit to find your "leaky bucket" expenses

- A challenge to build your first $100 in small wins

- Tools to recover after you "mess up" without spiraling

- A one-page dashboard you'll actually want to use

- Simple ways to rebuild the story you tell yourself about money

- An emergency plan for when financial crises hit

- Scripts for money conversations that don't end in meltdowns

- How to build a support system that sustains your progress

You'll also get stories from real people who used small resets to reconnect with their finances and rebuild confidence, one action at a time.

This Is a Book You Come Back To

This isn't something you read once and "finish."

It's something you return to when you:

- Fall behind

- Avoid your finances for weeks

- Overspend and want to hide

- Forget your progress and need a quick win

- Feel ready to go deeper

Every chapter ends with a micro action—a five-minute move that helps you interrupt avoidance, reduce shame, and reconnect with the future you're building.

One Promise Before We Begin

You will mess up again. You will forget to track something. You will have tough weeks and want to avoid it all.

When that happens, this book is your soft place to land. You don't start over. You **reset**.

That's what creates long-term success. Not perfection. But the identity of someone who always comes back.

You don't need a financial makeover. You need five minutes, one action, and a new belief:

"I can still move forward—even from here."

Let's begin.

SECTION 1:
RESET YOUR RELATIONSHIP WITH MONEY

Calm the chaos, interrupt avoidance, and normalize the ADHD-money struggle.

Chapter 1: The ADHD-Money Collision

Why Smart People Still Struggle with Their Finances

You can be brilliant, creative, hardworking—and still feel like your finances are a disaster.

This isn't because you're lazy. Or because you "just need a budget." It's because **ADHD and money collide in invisible, exhausting ways.**

What Nobody Told You About ADHD and Finances

If you live with ADHD, managing money doesn't just feel hard. It feels overwhelming, emotional, and sometimes impossible.

You might recognize these patterns:

- You avoid looking at accounts until something bounces

- You overspend impulsively, then feel deep regret

- You miss bills or due dates, even when you have the money

- You start tracking expenses—then abandon it after two days

- You feel like you can't trust yourself with money

These aren't character flaws. They're **functional symptoms** of how your brain processes time, emotion, and executive tasks.

The ADHD-Money Loop

Here's what typically happens:

1. You make a financial mistake (late bill, overdraft, big purchase)

2. You feel shame or panic

3. You avoid checking accounts because it's "too much"

4. Avoidance creates more chaos

5. The chaos confirms your belief: *"I'm bad with money"*

This loop reinforces **financial learned helplessness—** where you stop trying because every attempt seems doomed.

But here's the truth: You're not failing because you can't manage money. You're struggling because traditional money management **wasn't built for your brain.**

Why Typical Financial Advice Doesn't Work

Most personal finance systems assume you can:

- Track everything daily
- Plan months ahead
- Delay gratification without stress
- Stay consistent under pressure
- Manage small tasks without forgetting

ADHD disrupts all of that. We deal with:

- **Time blindness** (due dates sneak up or disappear)
- **Working memory gaps** (systems don't "stick")
- **Task initiation issues** (even small actions feel heavy)
- **Emotional reactivity** (money triggers shut us down)
- **Shame loops** (believing we "should be better" by now)

My Breaking Point

I remember sitting at my kitchen table, staring at my phone. I had my banking app open but couldn't bring myself to tap it.

The balance wasn't even the issue. It was the **feeling**—the tension in my chest, the shame in my gut, the voice whispering, *"If you were responsible, you wouldn't be here again."*

I wasn't broke. I wasn't reckless. But I was **disconnected**—from my money, my numbers, and myself.

So I did something strange. I didn't close the app. I didn't try to fix anything. I just kept it open and took a breath.

That was my first money reset. And it changed everything.

Real Story: Tara's Avoidance Spiral

Tara is a 35-year-old freelance web designer with ADHD. She makes decent money—but she never seems to know where it goes. She avoids her bank account, leaves invoices untracked, and defaults to credit cards during every crisis.

Every few months, she tells herself she'll "get it together." She downloads a budgeting app, tries for a few days, gets overwhelmed, and quits.

Eventually she stopped trying altogether—until a bounced rent payment forced her to look. Her anxiety was through the roof.

We didn't start with budgeting. We started with one simple reset: **Open the account. Breathe. That's enough for today.**

That reset was the doorway to a full transformation. But it had to start with safety—not shame.

What This Book Offers

This is not a budgeting manual. It's a **reset manual**— built specifically for ADHD brains that feel stuck, overwhelmed, or ashamed.

Every chapter gives you:

- **One five-minute action** to rebuild clarity or control

- **Realistic examples** of how ADHD brains can succeed without pressure

- **Zero shame-based language**

- **Clear prompts and checklists**

- **Repeatable systems** that build momentum without burnout

You don't need to overhaul your finances. You just need a path back into the game—one small reset at a time.

What You'll Learn in the Chapters Ahead

In this book, you'll learn how to:

- Open avoided accounts without panic

- Cancel money leaks and get your power back

- Track small wins instead of overwhelming spreadsheets

- Build reward budgets that keep you on track

- Create systems that work when your motivation doesn't

- Redefine your earning identity and rebuild financial trust

- Reset after financial mess-ups without spiraling into shame

- Navigate crises and difficult conversations with confidence

- Build support systems that sustain your progress

This is not a magic cure. It's a **daily micro-reset system** that gently rewires how you approach your money.

And it works. Not because it's hard. But because it's *built for the way you work.*

Key Takeaway

You're not bad with money. You've just never had a system that meets your brain where it is.

What to Do Next

Start where you are. The first reset isn't about fixing anything. It's about **noticing** where you've shut down—and choosing to re-engage, gently.

You're not broken. You just need a different approach. Let's take the next step together—one small reset at a time.

Chapter 2: What Is a Money Reset?

Small Wins. Big Shifts. Built for Real Brains.

Until my ADHD diagnosis, my money strategy was built on panic and overcorrection.

Ignore → feel guilty → binge budget → crash → repeat.

Every time I messed up, I'd try to overhaul everything:

- Color-coded spreadsheets
- Budgeting apps I never opened
- Financial podcasts I couldn't keep up with

I was chasing control in a system that wasn't built for my brain.

The idea of a "reset" didn't come from a book. It came from desperation. I needed **a way back in** that didn't feel like punishment.

What a Money Reset Really Means

A **money reset** is not a budget. It's not a plan. It's not a system you build when you finally "get your life together."

A reset is a short, intentional action that reconnects you with your finances—without shame, stress, or spreadsheets.

It's a small move that says: *"I'm not avoiding this anymore. I'm returning—even just for a moment."*

It can be:

- Opening your account, even if you don't look at numbers

- Canceling one unused subscription

- Writing down one thing you bought today

- Moving $5 to savings—just to prove you can

A reset doesn't require motivation. It doesn't require a clear head. It just requires **one moment of engagement**.

For ADHD brains like mine, that's the only place real progress begins.

The Moment That Changed the Model

I remember the exact moment I discovered the power of resets.

I was sitting at my kitchen table, paralyzed by the thought of opening my banking app. My chest was tight. My breathing was shallow. The voice in my head was screaming about how irresponsible I was.

But instead of closing my phone and walking away— which I'd done dozens of times before—I did something different.

I kept the app open and just breathed. I didn't check the balance. I didn't review transactions. I just sat with the app open and took five deep breaths.

That was it. That was my first reset.

And something shifted. Not in my bank account—but in my **relationship with my bank account**. I proved to myself that I could be present with my finances, even when it felt scary.

That 30-second action became the foundation for everything that followed.

Why This Works for the Way We're Wired

ADHD isn't about lack of willpower. It's about how our brains process time, emotion, and effort.

We struggle with:

- **Initiation** (we want to act, but can't start)

- **Working memory** (we forget we made a plan)

- **Dopamine regulation** (we need quick wins or we disengage)

- **Emotional avoidance** (if it feels bad, we run)

- **Shame spirals** (we assume struggle is personal failure)

When traditional advice tells us to "just make a budget and stick to it," it's like handing someone who's drowning a spreadsheet.

What we need isn't more structure. We need **a reset point**—a pattern interrupt we can return to, over and over, no matter how messy things feel.

A True Story: Jess and the Credit Card She Couldn't Look At

Jess is a creative entrepreneur who came to me after spiraling for months. She hadn't checked her credit card balance since the holidays. She told herself she'd do it "when she felt strong enough." That day never came.

What we did instead was simple: We sat side by side, and I asked her to open the app. Not to pay anything. Not to review every charge. Just. Open. It.

She did. She held her breath. And then she exhaled.

That moment—just clicking into the thing she feared—was the start of her financial healing.

Over the next few weeks, she didn't build a perfect system. But she kept resetting. She checked her balance every Sunday. She tracked one expense a day. She paid a little more than the minimum.

By the end of the month, she told me: *"I don't feel scared of money anymore. I feel like I'm in motion."*

Reset vs. Overhaul

Let's make this distinction very clear:

Overhaul Thinking	Reset Thinking
"I need to fix everything now"	"I'll take one small step today"
"This has to be perfect"	"This just needs to move me forward"
"I'll do it when I have time"	"I can do something in five minutes"
"I already failed, why bother?"	"Every day is a chance to reset"

Overhauls lead to burnout. **Resets lead to belief.**

And belief is the only thing that turns a pattern into a habit.

What Happens When You Start Resetting

You start to:

- Rebuild your financial **confidence**
- Create momentum with **micro-wins**

- Learn that **progress doesn't require perfection**

- Rewire your nervous system to stay calm around money

- Begin identifying as someone who *shows up*, not someone who hides

This is how you exit the shame spiral. Not by "doing better." But by **returning**, gently, one reset at a time.

Your First Resets (Pick One Today)

These aren't tests. They're invitations:

• **The Open & Breathe Reset** Open your bank app. Don't check numbers. Just breathe while it's open.

• **The Cancel One Thing Reset** Find one recurring charge you don't use. Cancel it. Reclaim that money.

• **The One Transaction Reset** Write down one thing you bought today. No judgment. Just notice it.

• **The $5 Confidence Reset** Move $5 to savings. Even if it's symbolic. Prove you take care of your future self.

What Resets Build Over Time

Every reset is:

- A step toward visibility

- A moment of identity change

- A message to your nervous system: *"We're okay. You can engage."*

Five minutes a day, over 30 days? That's not 150 minutes of effort. That's 30 *identity shifts.*

Those shifts are what make someone go from *"I'm bad with money"* to *"I'm rebuilding something strong."*

My Personal Reset Evolution

Today, three years after that first kitchen table moment, my relationship with money is completely different.

I still have challenging financial days. I still make mistakes. But I no longer disappear when things get hard.

Instead, I reset. I return to the practices that ground me:

- Opening my accounts calmly

- Tracking one transaction daily

- Moving small amounts to savings

- Celebrating micro-wins

- Treating setbacks as temporary

These aren't just financial habits. They're **identity practices**—daily proof that I'm someone who shows up, even when it's hard.

Key Takeaway

You don't need to be ready. You just need a way back in. A money reset is that way.

What to Do Next

Pick your first reset from the list above. Complete it today. Not because you're fixing anything—but because you're *reconnecting*.

Write it down. Feel the shift. And tomorrow, reset again.

The goal isn't perfection.

The goal is presence.

And presence, like everything else in this book, is a practice you can develop—one reset at a time.

Chapter 3: The Avoided Account Audit

Face the Numbers Without Fear

There was a time when opening my bank account felt like unlocking a vault I wasn't prepared to face.

I'd hover my thumb over the app, chest tight, already imagining the worst: *Maybe the balance is lower than I thought. Maybe a bill bounced. Maybe I forgot something again.*

Instead of checking, I'd close the app. Tell myself I'd look tomorrow.

But tomorrow didn't come. Not until something forced it.

That pattern repeated more times than I can count. Every time I avoided my money, I felt less in control. Less capable. Less like someone who could ever be financially confident.

The breakthrough didn't come from discipline. It came from a reset—what I now call the **Avoided Account Audit**.

Why We Avoid the Numbers

People with ADHD avoid financial information not because we don't care—but because our nervous system gets **flooded by it**.

Here's what's happening behind the scenes:

- We fear what we'll find, so we *don't look*

- We feel shame about what we *think* we'll see

- We catastrophize small unknowns into imagined disasters

- We've made money mistakes before—and assume we're still that person

- We think we need to fix everything once we open it... so we delay opening it at all

This is emotional overload—not irresponsibility. And avoidance becomes its own habit.

That's what we're breaking in this chapter.

What an Avoided Account Really Represents

It's never just about the money.

Avoiding an account often means avoiding:

- The emotional reaction we think it will trigger

- The story we've told ourselves about what it means

- The fear that if we *see it*, we'll feel even more stuck

But here's what's true: **Your account doesn't hold judgment. It holds information.**

And information, when seen calmly, becomes power.

The Power of Looking (Without Acting)

One of the most radical resets you can do is simply look. Not fix. Not organize. Just look.

This counters the ADHD brain's instinct to wait until we feel "ready"—which often means we never engage at all.

Looking breaks the avoidance loop. Looking creates emotional distance between the number and the story. Looking builds **financial object permanence**— the ability to hold truth without reacting to it.

Once you can look, you can lead.

The 5-Minute Audit Reset (Step-by-Step)

You don't need to prepare for this. You just need to start.

Step 1: Make a Short List of Accounts You Avoid

This could include:

- Checking accounts
- Credit cards
- PayPal/Venmo/Cash App
- Subscription platforms
- Investment or retirement accounts

You only need 3-5. No pressure to cover everything.

Step 2: Choose One to Open

Not all of them. Just one. The one that feels *least* terrifying—or the one you've avoided longest.

Step 3: Open It. That's It.

Don't fix anything. Don't analyze. Just open it and sit with whatever is there.

If that's all you do today, it's enough.

Step 4: Log the Emotional Reaction

Use a simple color code:

- Green: Neutral
- Yellow: Uncomfortable but manageable
- Orange: Tense or anxious

- Red: Flooded or frozen

This tracks your growth over time—not your financial stats, but your *emotional capacity*.

Step 5: Record One Note

Just write one reflection:

- "I thought it would be worse"

- "I felt frozen, but I did it"

- "I avoided this for a week and survived the truth"

That's the new habit: see → feel → name → reset.

What This Builds Over Time

The more you return to your accounts with gentleness, the more you teach your brain it's safe to look.

You prove that:

- You're capable of facing hard things

- You don't need a perfect system to stay connected

- You don't need to feel ready—you just need to return

Returning, over and over, is what breaks the loop of avoidance.

My Personal Audit Ritual

Today, my reset ritual is this:

- Sunday morning

- One cup of coffee

- I open three accounts and log balances

- I highlight one micro win

- I take a deep breath

It takes less than five minutes. But it took months of gentle resets to get there.

You don't have to start where I am. You just have to start where *you* are.

Key Takeaway

Avoidance keeps you anxious. Awareness sets you free.

What to Do Next

- Choose one account you've been avoiding

- Open it—even if you don't look at numbers

- Log how it felt (color or scale)

- Write one sentence about what you noticed

That's the audit. That's the win. No spreadsheets. No perfection. Just presence.

You've now done what most people never do: You faced your finances—and reclaimed your power.

Chapter 4: Track One Transaction

The Most Powerful Five Seconds in Your Financial Reset

There was a time when I couldn't remember what I spent money on yesterday.

I wasn't being careless. My brain just... didn't hold the information. It moved too fast, already thinking three steps ahead—or spiraling three steps behind.

If someone asked me, "How much did you spend on food last week?" I would've laughed. Not because I thought it was funny, but because even *knowing* that felt ridiculous.

That's how disconnected I was from my money.

It's also how I discovered something that changed everything: Tracking one transaction—just one—can reconnect you to your finances faster than any budget ever could.

The ADHD Disconnect

For most people with ADHD, money doesn't vanish because of irresponsibility. It vanishes because of **invisibility**.

We swipe a card and the brain moves on. We click "Buy Now" and forget we bought something. We get a receipt, toss it, and feel no difference in our bank balance... until we do.

It's not that we're not trying. It's that ADHD disrupts *working memory*, *object permanence*, and *delayed feedback*—all critical for traditional budgeting.

Which is why most financial advice doesn't work for us.

The Power of a Single Transaction

So what does work?

Slowing down. Capturing one moment. Creating **micro-visibility** in a financial life that otherwise feels abstract.

When you track a single transaction, you:

- Interrupt the autopilot loop

- Make your spending *real*—in a way your brain can hold

- Rebuild connection between behavior and awareness

- Shift from shame to curiosity

That single moment becomes a touchstone. A reference point.

"I spent $18 on lunch today" might not change your finances today, but it *changes your relationship with them.*

Real Story: My Visibility Reset

I tried comprehensive expense tracking for years. I'd use apps for a week, then ghost them because they made me feel worse.

So I flipped the goal. Instead of tracking everything, I challenged myself: **Write down one thing you bought each day. No totals. No categories. Just the item. Just the date.**

I did it on a sticky note by my bed. And something shifted.

After two weeks, I realized my daily coffee was the *only* thing I'd written down consistently.

It made me see how often I was escaping with spending. But without judgment. Just... awareness.

That's the beginning of change. Not restriction. **Reflection.**

The 5-Second Reset

Let me break this down:

Track One Transaction = 5 Seconds of Attention + 1 Moment of Power

That's it.

You don't need to:

- Categorize it

- Log it into a budgeting app

- Justify it

- Feel bad about it

You just need to **notice it. Name it.**

It's that micro-moment of observation that begins to rebuild **object permanence**—so your money no longer disappears behind brain fog.

Why This Works for ADHD Brains

Tracking one transaction:

- Creates **dopamine** through micro-achievement

- Builds **self-trust** by reinforcing the identity: *"I notice. I track."*

- Helps counteract **time blindness**, giving you a stronger internal clock

- Reduces financial **avoidance paralysis** because you're not trying to track *everything*—just one thing

It's the opposite of overwhelm. It's the re-entry point.

But What If I Forget?

Good. That means you're human.

Here's how to ADHD-proof this:

- **Habit stack it**: Track after brushing teeth, making coffee, or shutting down work

- **Set a reminder**: Phone alarm titled "One Thing I Bought Today"

- **Keep it visible**: Sticky note on your wallet, tracker in your planner

- **Make it analog**: Don't wait for the perfect app. A napkin works fine.

The Reset Tracker (Simple Format)

Here's the layout I still use when things feel scattered:

Date	What I Bought	Amount
Apr 20	Lunch - Bento Box	$13.50
Apr 21	Spotify Subscription	$9.99
Apr 22	Late-night snacks	$7.25

That's it. No overthinking. No perfect categories. Just awareness. Just connection.

Over time, you'll start seeing your own patterns. Not from shame—but from *truth*.

My Personal Ritual

There are days when I still feel the urge to check out. When spending feels automatic. When logging in feels too heavy.

So I bring it back to one thing. At night, I ask: *What did I spend money on today?*

Whether it was $2 or $200, I write it down. Not to punish myself. But to prove I'm still connected. Still present. Still building something stronger.

Key Takeaway

You don't need to track everything. You just need to start noticing something.

What to Do Next

Track **one** thing you bought today.

It could be:

- A subscription you forgot about

- A snack you grabbed at the gas station

- A purchase you made online this morning

Write it down. That's it. That's your reset.

Repeat tomorrow. And the day after. Let the habit of attention turn into a habit of confidence.

One transaction at a time.

SECTION 2:
BUILD YOUR RESET SYSTEM

Equip yourself with concrete tools to take back control—without the overwhelm

Chapter 5: Find Your Leaky Bucket

Stop the Drip Before You Try to Fill It

I wasn't just "bad at saving." I was trying to pour money into a bucket that had holes in the bottom.

It didn't matter how much I earned. It didn't matter how motivated I felt. If the leaks were still open—subscriptions I forgot, small charges I didn't track, upgrades I didn't need—**everything I poured in would eventually leak out.**

And I didn't even notice it happening.

The ADHD Money Leak

Here's what you need to know: Most ADHD money leaks are small. That's why they fly under the radar.

- $9.99 a month for a forgotten app

- $14.99 for a streaming service you use once monthly

- $6.49 for "rush" delivery you didn't need

- $3.00 tip defaults you forgot to adjust

- $1.29 in auto-updated cloud storage you never review

Individually? These charges seem harmless. But stacked? They add up to *hundreds* or even *thousands* of dollars a year.

More importantly: They keep you feeling like your money just... disappears.

Why We Don't Catch These Leaks

People with ADHD struggle with:

- **Object permanence** (If we're not seeing it, we're not thinking about it)

- **Subscription amnesia** (We sign up during motivation... then forget)

- **Overwhelm paralysis** (We want to fix it all, so we fix nothing)

- **Micro-shame** ("It's just $5, I should be more responsible")

- **Decision fatigue** (We don't review because *choosing what to cancel* is exhausting)

But here's the truth: You don't need a perfect budget. You just need to **plug the holes** before you try to save more.

The Bucket Metaphor

Imagine trying to fill a bucket with water. But every time you pour more in, it drips out through tiny cracks.

Would your first move be to pour faster? Or would you patch the holes?

Exactly.

Your finances are the same.

Even if you don't make more money, even if you don't change your income right now—**plugging the leaks gives you instant relief.**

This is where confidence begins.

My Leak Discovery

One particularly frustrating month, I couldn't figure out why I felt broke despite making decent money. I did a simple leak audit and found:

- $21.99/month for a design app I hadn't used in six months

- $12.99 for a meditation app I forgot I had

- $9.99 for premium Spotify my ex was still using

- $4.99 for an old magazine subscription that charged yearly

That was over $50/month. I canceled three things that week. I didn't feel deprived. I felt **powerful**.

How to Find Your Leaks (Without Overwhelm)

Let's keep this reset small, sharp, and doable.

Step 1: Choose One Account to Review

Pick a place where recurring charges happen:

- Your bank account
- Credit card
- App store
- PayPal or Venmo
- Email receipts folder

You only need to look at **1-2 months** of activity.

Step 2: Scan for Sneaky Recurring Charges

Look for:

- Streaming services
- Monthly apps
- Software you've outgrown
- Donation auto-charges
- Trial sign-ups you forgot to cancel

- Yearly renewals you didn't see coming

Make a list. Don't judge. Just capture.

Step 3: Create a Quick "Leak Table"

Service/Expense	Monthly Cost	Keep It?	Annual Savings if Canceled
Streaming Service A	$14.99	No	$179.88
Cloud Storage	$9.99	Yes	-
Dating App Premium	$19.99	No	$239.88

This is not about judgment. It's about **visibility**.

What Plugging Leaks Does for You

- It stops financial "slow drains" that keep you stuck

- It gives you **instant wins**—small amounts that feel big emotionally

- It helps reframe your identity from *reactive* to *resourceful*

- It builds **momentum**—because once you cancel one thing, it gets easier to cancel two

- It reintroduces **choice**—you get to decide where your money goes

Even canceling one forgotten subscription can reset your sense of control.

My Monthly Leak Ritual

Once a month, I scan just one account—usually my credit card. I check for anything I don't recognize, don't use, or don't need anymore.

Sometimes I cancel something. Sometimes I just notice a trend (like takeout spikes). Sometimes I do nothing but observe.

The point isn't to catch everything. The point is to *stay connected*. And that connection? It changes your whole financial story.

Key Takeaway

You don't need to earn more. You just need to stop the silent leaks.

What to Do Next

1. Pick one place to check—bank, card, app store, PayPal

2. Find one recurring charge you forgot about

3. Decide: Keep it? Cancel it? Review it next month?

4. Cancel it if it's no longer serving you

5. Write down what you just saved

That's your reset. And it's worth more than the dollars. It's about reclaiming the role of **money leader**—not money avoider.

You're not "bad with money." You're just beginning to look more closely.

Chapter 6: Create a Spending Reset Ritual

Pause Before You Swipe—Without Shame

ADHD spending isn't always impulsive. Sometimes it's emotional. Sometimes it's survival. Sometimes it's just... unconscious.

You might not realize you're spending until:

- You see a charge on your account

- The package shows up

- Or your card declines at checkout

You didn't mean to sabotage your goals. You weren't trying to blow the budget. You just... *reacted.*

That's what this chapter is here to change.

A **Spending Reset Ritual** helps you:

- Slow the loop

- Insert awareness

- Make space for choice

- Create a *moment of power* before the purchase

Not a rule. Not a punishment. A pause.

Why ADHD Brains Struggle with Spending Regulation

This is *not* about being irresponsible. Here's what's really happening:

- **Low dopamine drive** → Seeking stimulation or "feel good" hits

- **Emotional dysregulation** → Spending as comfort or escape

- **Time blindness** → "I deserve this now," without seeing future impact

- **All-or-nothing thinking** → "I already blew my budget, might as well..."

- **Decision fatigue** → Easier to click *Buy Now* than think through consequences

This is why traditional budgeting doesn't fix the problem. You need a **pre-spending pattern interrupt—** something built for how your brain actually works.

How a Sticky Note Saved Me Hundreds

There was a time when I'd open shopping apps *automatically* when anxious. I wasn't looking for anything particular. I just needed a hit of control, of agency, of something that felt good.

One day, I stuck a note on my laptop that said: "Pause. What do I really need right now?"

I didn't stop spending overnight. But that tiny moment of awareness stopped dozens of transactions over the next few months.

Because the spending wasn't the problem. The *unconsciousness* was.

Step-by-Step: Build Your Spending Reset Ritual

This is not about control. It's about **conscious choice**.

Step 1: Identify Your Spending Triggers

Ask yourself:

- When am I most likely to spend impulsively?

- What emotional state leads me to shop?

- What apps or stores feel most "automatic"?

Examples:

- Late-night scrolling

- After a stressful workday

- While avoiding tasks

- When overwhelmed, bored, or lonely

Awareness = power.

Step 2: Choose a 60-90 Second Interrupt Ritual

Pick something **physical, sensory, or visible.**

Ideas:

- Light a candle
- Take 3 deep breaths
- Put your phone down and stretch
- Write what you want to buy on a sticky note
- Say a reset phrase out loud
- Look at your financial priority tracker

You're not trying to suppress the desire. You're giving it room to breathe.

Step 3: Use a Reset Phrase

Keep one of these somewhere visible—or memorize your favorite:

"Pause. I get to choose." "My future self is watching—and cheering me on." "Is this relief or reward?" "I don't need to decide now. I can wait 10 minutes." "A reset is not a restriction—it's a return to power."

You can also write your own.

Step 4: Add a Delay Window

Most impulse urges lose steam after 10-15 minutes. Give your brain a chance to rebalance.

Try:

- Setting a timer

- Taking a short walk

- Switching to a different task

- Adding the item to a "Buy Later" list

Often, the craving passes—and your confidence *spikes.*

Know Your Spending Personality

Different ADHD brains struggle with different patterns. Match your strategy to your style.

The Emotional Buyer Spends when anxious, lonely, or overwhelmed *Your ritual:* Comfort cue + breathwork before checkout

The Dopamine Seeker Spends out of boredom or craving stimulation *Your ritual:* Delay window + reward replacement (walk, call friend)

The Avoider Spends to avoid tasks, emotions, or responsibilities *Your ritual:* Pause + micro-action (check balance, delete 1 tab)

Why This Works for ADHD Brains

- Creates a *pattern interrupt* before the reward loop kicks in

- Adds **choice and intention** where there was only reaction

- Puts control *in your body*, not just your mind

- Builds a **repeatable ritual** your nervous system will recognize and trust

You don't have to stop spending completely. You just need to *reset the moment*—so the action is yours, not automatic.

Key Takeaway

ADHD-driven spending is often emotional, unconscious, or stress-triggered. A 60-90 second ritual helps you interrupt the loop before money leaves your account.

What to Do Next

Build your Spending Reset Ritual today:

1. Pick a trigger you want to interrupt

2. Create a 2-minute ritual (breath + phrase + delay)

3. Try it once this week

That pause? That's where power lives.

Chapter 7: Automate One Thing

Make Progress Without Willpower

There was a period when I was doing everything manually. I paid bills manually. I moved money to savings manually. I reminded myself—manually—to check balances, track subscriptions, and pay down debt.

I thought that was responsible. What it really was... was exhausting.

Every single financial task became a decision. And every decision became a potential failure point.

Because when you live with ADHD, **relying on memory or motivation is a gamble**. Some days you're on top of everything. Other days, brushing your teeth feels like a win.

I didn't need to try harder. I needed a system that would work when I couldn't.

That's when I made one of the most life-changing shifts in my money journey. I stopped managing everything—and started **automating one thing at a time.**

Why Automation Is a Reset Superpower

For ADHD brains, automation is more than convenience. It's a lifeline.

Because when you:

- Struggle to initiate tasks

- Forget dates or skip steps

- Live in emotional and mental overload

- Burn out from doing too much at once

...what you really need is a **system that runs without needing you.**

Automation takes tasks off your plate **permanently,** reducing:

- Decision fatigue

- Late payments

- Forgetting to save

- Guilt and shame around inconsistent habits

You don't need to automate everything. You just need to **automate one thing**—and let it do the work for you.

The 5-Minute Money Reset

What You Can Automate (Start Small)

Task	Automation Method
Paying bills on time	Set up autopay with due date reminders
Building emergency fund	Weekly auto-transfer to savings
Paying down credit cards	Recurring payment of minimum or fixed amount
Separating tax money	% of income auto-routed to tax savings
Funding reward account	$5/week to "Fun Money" fund
Budgeting with guardrails	Auto-transfers to separate spending account

You don't need to do all of this. You just need to **choose one thing.**

How to Choose Your First Automation

Ask yourself:

1. **What do I always forget to do?** Bills, savings, credit payments?

2. **What do I dread doing?** Transferring money? Deciding what to save?

3. **What would feel amazing if it just... happened?** Imagine waking up and realizing money moved while you slept.

Then pick one.

The 5-Minute Reset Setup

Let's walk through it:

1. **Log into your bank or payment app**

2. Choose a target: savings, bill, card, or fund

3. Set up a **recurring transfer or payment:**

   o Weekly (small savings)

   o Biweekly (after paydays)

   o Monthly (fixed bills or card paydown)

4. Label the automation something empowering ("Freedom Fund," "Future Me," "Stress-Free Rent")

5. Hit confirm

You've just created a system that moves money without asking your brain for permission every time.

My Automation Stack

These are the automations that changed my life:

- $25 every Friday to savings

- $10/week to my "rewards fund"

- Automatic credit card minimum payment (no more late fees)

- Biweekly transfer to a "buffer" account I treat like it doesn't exist

None of these are huge amounts. But together, they've created something far more valuable than money: **Stability.**

A Note on ADHD Resistance to Autopay

You might be thinking: "But what if the money isn't there? What if something goes wrong?"

That's fair. Here's what I recommend:

- Start with a **low-risk automation** (small savings, fixed bill)

- Set a **calendar reminder** to check in weekly

- Keep a "cancel anytime" policy—this is a tool, not a trap

The point is not to set it and forget forever. The point is to **set it and stop relying on memory**.

Once your confidence grows, you can add more later.

Key Takeaway

When your motivation drops, automation takes over. That's how progress becomes inevitable.

What to Do Next

1. Choose one thing to automate this week:

    o   A $5 transfer to savings

    o   A fixed bill that's due every month

    o   A credit card minimum payment

2. Log in. Set it up.

3. Add a reminder to check in next week and see how it went.

You've just created your first automatic money win. And the best part? You don't have to "stay on track."

The track now runs without you.

Chapter 8: Build Your Reward Budget

Fuel Your Progress with What Feels Good

For most of my life, I thought saving money meant cutting off anything that felt fun.

No takeout. No little splurges. No last-minute coffees or Friday sushi runs.

I was trying to be disciplined. But really, I was swinging between two extremes:

All restriction (spend nothing, feel deprived) and **All impulse** (spend everything, feel out of control)

It was unsustainable. More than that—it was demoralizing. Because every time I tried to "be good with money," I lost access to joy.

Until I did something I'd never done before. I gave myself **permission to enjoy my money**—but with structure. Not guilt. Not chaos. Structure.

I built something called a **reward budget**. And it changed everything.

Why ADHD Brains Need Built-In Rewards

Most personal finance books preach delayed gratification. That might work for neurotypical brains with strong internal clocks and consistent dopamine regulation.

But for ADHD brains, **"I'll reward myself later" doesn't always land.**

Here's why:

- ADHD brains are dopamine-deficient—we need hits of pleasure or novelty to stay motivated

- We often lose track of long-term goals, even ones we care about

- We associate "good money behavior" with deprivation, punishment, or restriction

- When we finally burn out? We splurge just to feel alive again

That's not a lack of discipline. That's an unmet neurological need.

The Power of the Reward Budget

A **reward budget** is a separate fund you create **specifically for joy**—for small, guilt-free spending that actually reinforces your good habits.

It's not a loophole. It's part of the system.

It tells your brain: "When I stay connected to my finances, I get to feel good—not deprived."

That's how you build long-term consistency. Not by removing all joy. But by giving yourself joy that's earned, planned, and celebrated.

How to Build Your Own Reward Budget

Let's keep this simple.

Step 1: Choose an Amount That Feels Light and Consistent

This could be:

- $5 a week

- $10 every payday

- A percentage of your income (1-3%)

It doesn't have to be big. It just has to be **visible and repeatable**.

Step 2: Set Up a Separate Place for It

Open a new account. Or use a cash envelope. Or label it in your budgeting app as "Fun Fund," "Joy Jar," or "Dopamine Dollars."

Name it something that makes your brain smile. This is your *permission slip* fund.

Step 3: Link It to a Habit (Optional)

You don't have to earn it through pain. But you can link it to a reset.

Examples:

- Every time you do a weekly money check-in, $5 goes into the reward fund

- Every time you track transactions for five days straight

- Every time you show up—even if you didn't do everything perfectly

Make the reward part of the rhythm, not the escape from it.

What Can You Spend It On?

Whatever makes you feel:

- Celebrated

- Recharged

- Connected to your joy

Examples:

- A fancy coffee or your favorite snack

- A new pen, journal, book, or playlist subscription

- A self-care treat or mini adventure

- A small item that supports a hobby or creative outlet

The key is this: **It's guilt-free. It's planned. And it tells your nervous system, "You did something right."**

Why This Changes Everything

When you build a reward budget:

- You **reframe saving** from deprivation to empowerment

- You reinforce the identity: *"I'm someone who shows up for my money and myself"*

- You create **built-in relief valves** so you don't binge spend later

- You turn **money rituals into something your brain actually craves**

That craving? That's what fuels consistency.

My Reward Budget Ritual

Every Friday, $10 hits my "Freedom Fund."

Some weeks I use it on a long walk with my favorite overpriced smoothie. Other weeks it stacks up for a month and I buy myself something I've been eyeing—guilt-free.

But every time I use it, I think: "This came from me showing up. This joy is earned."

That feeling makes it easier to keep showing up.

Key Takeaway

Discipline doesn't have to feel like punishment. When you reward yourself on purpose, consistency becomes a pleasure—not a prison.

What to Do Next

1. Choose your **weekly reward amount** ($5-$10 is perfect to start)

2. Create a place for it (new account, envelope, jar, etc.)

3. Name it something fun

4. Decide: Will you link it to a reset or habit? Or just transfer it weekly no matter what?

Celebrate when you use it. That's not "breaking the rules." That's proof that the system is working.

Chapter 9: Pick One Financial Priority

Clarity Begins When You Stop Trying to Fix Everything

There was a moment early in my reset journey when I hit a wall—not because I wasn't trying, but because I was trying to do **everything at once.**

I had debt I wanted to pay down. Savings I wanted to build. Bills I was trying to catch up on. A credit score I couldn't even look at.

So, I did what most people with ADHD tend to do when faced with too many options: **Nothing.**

I froze.

Every financial task felt important. Every problem screamed for attention. And I couldn't decide what to focus on. So, I didn't focus on anything.

That's when I discovered the power of picking **one financial priority**—and letting everything else wait. Not forever. Just for now. Just long enough to let my brain breathe.

The ADHD Freeze Response

Let's be honest: ADHD isn't just about distraction. It's about **overload**.

Your brain isn't wired to hold 10 competing financial goals at once. And yet, when everything feels urgent—paying off debt, saving for emergencies, managing spending—you default to survival mode.

That means:

- Task paralysis

- All-or-nothing behavior

- Avoidance masked as "waiting for the right time"

- Stress that shuts down your executive function

This isn't laziness. It's neurological burnout.

And the cure isn't more effort. It's **simplifying your decision field** down to one clear path forward.

The Financial Focus Filter

Here's a simple tool to help you choose your next priority:

Ask: What's the ONE thing I could work on right now that would...

- Reduce my financial anxiety the fastest?

- Give me a quick win and build momentum?

- Make other decisions easier down the road?

- Align with what's most urgent (not just loudest)?

Then circle it. Commit to it. Let it lead.

Priority Examples (You Don't Have to Do Them All)

Priority Area	Why It Might Be Right for You
Build a Mini Emergency Fund	You're tired of surprises turning into chaos
Pay Off One Credit Card	You want to stop bleeding interest or rebuild trust
Cancel Unused Subscriptions	You need quick relief and instant control
Track Spending for 7 Days	You're overwhelmed and need clarity
Automate a Bill or Transfer	You keep forgetting and want stability
Boost Your Income	Your expenses are okay, but cash flow is tight

You're not choosing what's "right." You're choosing what's **next**.

My Priority Story

When I was drowning in decision paralysis, I picked the smallest thing that would give me the biggest emotional relief: **building a $500 emergency fund.**

Not because it was "the most strategic"—but because I was tired of panic when surprise bills hit.

Once I focused on that one thing, everything else quieted. Within two months, I had the fund. And more importantly, I had my **agency** back.

Not because I fixed everything. But because I didn't let the overwhelm define me.

Why This Works

When you choose one priority:

- Your brain can actually focus (instead of spinning)

- You build momentum through completion

- You prove to yourself that progress is possible

- You create clarity about what matters most

- Other problems often resolve themselves while you're focused

The goal isn't to ignore everything else forever. It's to give yourself **permission to focus** until this one thing is handled.

But What About Everything Else?

Write them down. Put them on a "Later List." Acknowledge they matter—but not *right now*.

When you finish your one priority, you can come back and pick the next one. But for now? Everything else can wait.

Because the cost of trying to do everything is doing nothing. And doing nothing guarantees you'll stay stuck.

Key Takeaway

You don't need to fix everything to fix something. Pick one priority and let it lead you forward.

What to Do Next

1. List all your financial concerns or goals

2. Use the Focus Filter to pick ONE priority

3. Write it down: "For the next 30 days, I'm focusing on _____"

4. Put everything else on a "Later List"

5. Take one small action toward your priority today

Scott Allan

You're not behind. You're just getting started. And starting with one thing is how everything changes.

Chapter 10: The $100 Reset Challenge

Build Belief with Every Dollar
You Reclaim

I still remember the first time I saved $100 on purpose.

Not from a paycheck. Not from something automatic. But from tracking tiny changes that added up to something real.

I'd been avoiding money for months, ashamed of the chaos inside. Then I challenged myself—not to get everything perfect, but to see if I could *build* $100 in small wins.

At the time, it felt like a joke. I didn't believe I had that much "extra" to find. But five minutes a day changed that.

Canceling a subscription here. Returning something I didn't need there. Selling an old mic. Making one better decision during a stressful day.

And just like that—I had $100.

But it wasn't the money that changed me. It was the **proof**: I was no longer stuck.

That's what this challenge is about.

Why $100 Is the Perfect ADHD-Sized Goal

For ADHD brains, big numbers feel abstract.

- "Save $10,000" sounds impossible

- "Pay off all your debt" sounds like a mountain

- "Fix your finances" sounds like a vague threat

But **$100**? It's clear. It's achievable. It feels real.

Most importantly:

- It gives you quick feedback

- It reinforces identity change ("I'm someone who can make progress")

- It activates your brain's reward system—every dollar becomes a win

- It helps you prove momentum is possible— even without a master plan

You don't need to feel ready. You just need to start.

How the $100 Reset Challenge Works

This isn't a budget. This is a **progress-tracking game**.

The 5-Minute Money Reset

You're building $100 through **doable wins**—not discipline. You're resetting your brain with every dollar you reclaim, save, or earn.

Step 1: Create a $100 Reset Tracker

Draw 10 boxes. Each box = $10. Color them in as you go, or use a spreadsheet, sticky notes, or a wall calendar.

You want to **see the progress** as it builds.

Step 2: Choose Your Method(s)

You can combine saving, earning, and canceling.

Method Examples

Save	Move $10 to savings, skip takeout, grocery swap
Cancel	Unused subscriptions, duplicate apps, auto-renewals
Earn	Sell unused gear, pick up a side gig, invoice faster

Each action gets logged. Each win gets counted. Every dollar builds belief.

Step 3: Keep It Visible

Put your tracker:

- On your fridge

- In your planner

- On your phone home screen

- On a sticky note you see every day

The more you see it, the more you'll engage with it.

What Counts as a Win?

Anything that gets you closer to the $100.

- Canceling a $12 subscription = +$12

- Returning a $25 unused Amazon item = +$25

- Selling something on Facebook Marketplace = +$30

- Choosing not to buy something = estimated savings = +$10

- Moving $5 to a "win fund" every day = +$35 by the end of a week

The point isn't how much—it's **why it matters**.

Each action says: "I'm not stuck. I'm still building."

Why This Works for ADHD Brains

- **Visual progress** keeps you motivated

- **Low pressure** keeps you out of shame

- **Small wins** give you dopamine

- **Quick actions** make it easier to stay engaged

- **Proving you can do it** shifts your identity

Once you finish your first $100 reset, you won't just believe you can do it again. You'll believe you're someone who *does* reset. That's the transformation.

My $100 Reset Ritual

I keep a running list in my phone. Every time I save, cancel, or choose better—I log the date, the action, and the dollar amount.

And I celebrate. Out loud. I'll say: "That's $6. Boom. I win again."

Because it's not about the amount. It's about the momentum.

Key Takeaway

Money confidence isn't built from big leaps. It's built from proving, over and over, that you can move forward.

What to Do Next

1. Draw or create your own $100 tracker (10 boxes = $10 each)

2. Save, cancel, or earn your first $5-$10

3. Log it. Count it. Celebrate it.

4. Repeat tomorrow

Finish your first $100 reset, and you'll finish the story you've been telling yourself: *"I can't manage money."*

Now, the new story begins: *"I reset. I rebuild. I move forward. And I can do it again."*

SECTION 3:
RESET YOUR BELIEFS AND BEHAVIORS

Strengthen emotional resilience, rebuild confidence, and create a sustainable rhythm.

Chapter 11: Make Your Weekly Money Reset

One Ritual. Five Minutes. Total Reconnection.

There was a time when I avoided looking at my finances for weeks. Not because I didn't care. But because every time I thought about it, I felt a jolt of panic.

A voice whispering, *"You're behind again. You messed up again. You'll never catch up."*

So, I did what a lot of ADHD brains do: **I avoided**.

But avoidance doesn't make the panic go away. It makes the problem grow in the dark.

I didn't need a spreadsheet. I didn't need to "budget harder." What I needed was a **safe, repeatable ritual**—something small, predictable, and shame-free.

That's when I started doing a **weekly money reset**. Five minutes. Once a week. Not to fix everything—just to reconnect.

Over time, that reset became my anchor.

Why Weekly Works for ADHD Brains

Here's why daily money tracking is often too much:

- It feels tedious

- We forget

- One missed day leads to a shame spiral

- Our executive function is already maxed out

And here's why monthly check-ins don't work either:

- Too much happens between check-ins

- We don't catch things in time

- It feels like "starting over" every month

Weekly resets are the sweet spot:

- They're frequent enough to stay current

- Short enough to not feel overwhelming

- Gentle enough to keep your nervous system calm

Think of it like brushing your financial teeth. A quick clean once a week prevents decay later.

What a Weekly Money Reset Looks Like

Here's what mine looks like—and how you can make it your own.

Step 1: Choose Your Energy Level

Each week is different. ADHD moods fluctuate. So don't force intensity. Adapt.

Energy Level	Reset Plan
Low Energy	Open your account. Breathe. Write down one win.
Moderate Energy	Check balances, skim transactions, log 1-2 notes
High Energy	Review dashboard, update budget, set a money goal

This removes pressure. No "perfect reset." Just presence.

Step 2: Use a Simple Framework

You can journal this, speak it out loud, or use a worksheet.

Here's a reset prompt structure:

- **This week's micro win:** (What did I do right?) *e.g., "Cancelled a $12 app," "Didn't impulse spend on Friday"*

- **This week's challenge:** (What threw me off?) *e.g., "Emotional day = retail therapy," "Forgot to log expenses"*

- **Next small action:** (What will I try this week?) *e.g., "Move $5 to savings," "Track 2 days of spending," "Automate 1 bill"*

- **Money mood check:** ☑ Calm ☑ Avoidant ☑ Overwhelmed ☑ Empowered

Naming your state creates self-awareness without shame.

Step 3: Set a Tiny Anchor Action

At the end of your reset, take one **micro-action** to complete the ritual.

Examples:

- Move $5 to savings

- Check your reward budget

- Send one invoice

- Track one expense

- Update one number on your dashboard

This tells your brain: "We don't just think about money—we take care of it."

Rituals That Make This Stick

ADHD thrives on **habit stacking**—linking one action to something you already do.

Ideas to build your weekly reset into your life:

- Pair it with Sunday coffee or Saturday laundry

- Use music, lighting, or a location to cue the reset

- Put it on your calendar as a recurring 10-minute appointment

- Stack it with a reward—reset first, then treat yourself

This isn't a chore. It's a check-in with your future self.

Why This Ritual Works

- Keeps your relationship with money **active but low-pressure**

- Builds **emotional regulation**—money doesn't scare you anymore

- Helps you **catch leaks or issues** before they grow

- Reinforces the identity: *"I show up for my money, even if it's messy."*

The ritual doesn't have to be fancy. It just has to be yours.

Key Takeaway

Money consistency doesn't start with spreadsheets. It starts with returning—even when you feel like hiding.

What to Do Next

1. Choose your reset day (Sunday, Monday— whatever feels good)

2. Block 10 minutes. Create a vibe—tea, music, calm.

3. Run through the reset:

   o Log one win

   o Log one challenge

   o Pick one small action

4. Repeat next week

Keep it light. Keep it flexible. Keep it yours. The ritual is how you reset your relationship with money. And it starts this week.

Chapter 12: Reset After a Money Mess-Up

You Didn't Fail—You Just Need a Way Back

Let me tell you something that used to derail me for *weeks*:

I'd have one "bad money day."

- I'd impulse buy something I didn't need

- Forget a bill

- Drain my account on UberEats after a long week

- Ignore a payment reminder because I couldn't deal emotionally

And then I'd think: *"Well, I blew it. I'll deal with it later."*

Later would turn into silence. Silence would turn into shame. And shame would turn into **avoidance**.

That one mistake became a story: *"You're bad with money. You always mess this up."*

Here's what I know now that I didn't know then: **Messing up isn't the problem. Staying stuck is.**

What you need most after a money mistake isn't punishment. It's **a reset**.

Why ADHD Brains Struggle With Mistakes

When you have ADHD, a small money mess-up doesn't just feel frustrating—it feels like proof.

Proof that you can't be trusted with money. Proof that all your progress was fake. Proof that you're "too scattered" or "too impulsive" or "too broken."

This happens because ADHD brains:

- Are wired for **all-or-nothing thinking**

- Experience **intensified rejection and self-criticism**

- Struggle to **emotionally separate now from next**

- Tend to over-identify with mistakes

That's why one bad day can make us disappear from our financial lives for weeks.

But here's the truth: A money mess-up is not a failure. It's an invitation. To return. To reset. To respond with **compassion and clarity**.

The 5-Minute Reset After a Mess-Up

When you make a money mistake (big or small), use this simple flow:

Step 1: Pause the Panic

Say out loud: *"This doesn't mean I've failed. It means I'm human."*

Breathe. Step away. Interrupt the spiral.

Step 2: Find the Fact

Look at the mistake directly, without adding a story.

- How much did you spend?

- What did you miss?

- What actually happened?

ADHD brains jump from action to identity. This step brings you back to neutral ground.

Step 3: Ask What Triggered It

Not to assign blame—but to increase awareness.

- Was I stressed?

- Was I overstimulated or under-stimulated?

- Did I need rest, not reward?

- Did I feel out of control and tried to buy it back?

Understanding the *why* is how you prevent shame from hijacking the reset.

Step 4: Take One Repair Action

Don't try to undo everything. Pick a single step that restores clarity or control.

Examples:

- Re-label a budget category

- Cancel one subscription to balance spending

- Re-engage with your tracker or reward fund

- Move $5 back to savings

- Reset your dashboard with new numbers

Step 5: Log a Lesson

Write down:

- "What did I learn?"

- "What can I try differently next time?"

- "What do I want to remember about this moment?"

This is how you transform regret into resilience.

Why This Reset Is a Game-Changer

When you handle money mess-ups with clarity and care:

- You stop reinforcing the identity of "I always screw this up"

- You build emotional regulation muscles

- You replace shame spirals with structured reentry

- You feel safer in your financial life—which makes you show up more often

Because if your financial system only works when you're perfect? It's not a system. It's a trap.

My Personal Reset Ritual

When I mess up—and I still do—I follow this three-sentence script:

"That was a hard moment. I'm still in control. I choose to return now."

Then I do something small:

- Open my dashboard

- Log the mistake without judgment

- Take one small action to move forward

That's the difference between shame and resilience: **a single action.**

Key Takeaway

A money mess-up is not the end. It's the middle. And you get to choose what happens next.

What to Do Next

1. Think of the last money mistake that made you spiral

2. Write down what actually happened (facts only)

3. Choose one micro repair action:

   o Move $5

   o Re-open a tracker

   o Forgive yourself out loud

4. Write down one lesson—not from punishment, but from *presence*

You didn't ruin your progress. You just hit a bump on a road you're still traveling.

And now, you reset.

Chapter 13: Break the Shame Loop

Stop Beating Yourself Up. Start Moving Forward.

There's something worse than any money mistake I ever made.

It wasn't a late payment. It wasn't over-drafting my account. It wasn't forgetting to check my bank balance for a month.

It was the **shame** that followed.

The looping, spiraling voice that told me: *"You did it again. You're irresponsible. You'll never change."*

And once that voice kicked in, I disappeared from my financial life for days. Sometimes weeks.

That's the shame loop. And it's one of the most toxic patterns that ADHD brains fall into—not just with money, but with everything we struggle to control.

But here's what I've learned, after years of facing it down: **Shame doesn't make you better. It keeps you stuck.**

This chapter is your reset point—not from mistakes, but from the self-punishment that follows.

What Is a Shame Loop?

A **shame loop** is a cycle that reinforces avoidance and paralysis after you make a mistake.

It usually goes something like this:

1. You mess up (spend impulsively, forget a payment, avoid your budget)

2. You feel deep guilt and embarrassment

3. You interpret the mistake as a reflection of who you are (*"I'm bad with money"*)

4. You avoid your finances to escape that feeling

5. That avoidance creates more chaos

6. The chaos confirms your shame

And the loop keeps going.

For ADHD brains, it's especially hard to break because:

- Our emotional regulation systems are more reactive

- We tie our performance to our worth

- We're used to feeling "behind" or "less than"

- We assume the mistake means we'll never get it right

This isn't just emotional. It's neurological. But it's not permanent.

Real Story: Leo and the Overdraft Spiral

Leo was a 35-year-old project manager who felt like a failure every time his account hit zero.

Even if it was just for a day. Even if it was caused by a timing issue.

He wouldn't log in for weeks after. He ignored his credit card notifications. And he stopped saving altogether.

Not because of money. Because of **shame**.

When we started working together, I asked him what he believed after those moments.

He said: *"It means I'm not someone who can be trusted with money."*

That belief had more power than the overdraft itself.

So we created a new pattern. After every slip-up, he practiced saying: *"This mistake is temporary. I'm still learning. I can return now."*

It felt fake at first. But slowly, his brain started to believe it.

He didn't stop messing up overnight. But he **stopped disappearing**. That's the real win.

Why Shame Doesn't Help You Change

Shame convinces you that:

- You're too far gone

- You need to hide to "fix it" before coming back

- You're not worthy of support, progress, or trust

But shame has **never paid off debt.** Shame has **never rebuilt a savings account.** Shame has **never helped you show up with calm and clarity.**

It only ever pulls you away from the very systems that could help you reset.

That's why **breaking the shame loop** is not emotional fluff. It's a critical step in your money reset system.

The 5-Minute Shame Reset (Interrupt the Loop)

Use this when you catch yourself spiraling after a money mistake.

Step 1: Name It Without Judgment

Say or write: *"I made a mistake, and I feel [ashamed, guilty, anxious, avoidant]."*

Naming it gives you emotional distance. It moves the shame from identity to experience.

Step 2: Interrupt the Story

What is your shame loop telling you?

"You'll never be good with money." "You always ruin your progress." "You're not meant to handle this."

Now replace it with a reset phrase: *"This is hard because of how my brain works—not because I'm broken."*

Step 3: Reconnect With the Present

Ask:

- What's the next small thing I can do right now?

- Can I open my account, even if I don't act?

- Can I write down one thing I *did* do well this week?

This is how you stop the loop: **through action—not perfection.**

What Breaking the Shame Loop Builds

When you practice this reset, you begin to:

- Trust yourself to come back faster

- Regulate your emotions after setbacks

- Separate your identity from your actions

- Build a safe internal system that doesn't rely on being "flawless"

This is where money confidence grows. Not from always doing it right. But from learning how to return with kindness.

My Go-To Reset Phrase

When I start to spiral, I say this out loud:

"This is just a mistake. I'm still the kind of person who shows up."

Then I do one small thing:

- Open my dashboard

- Cancel a charge

- Write down what I'm feeling

- Move $1 to savings just to prove I can

That tiny move interrupts the identity spiral. And I come back to myself.

The Shame Spiral vs. The Reset Spiral

Let me show you the difference:

Shame Spiral: Mistake → Self-attack → Avoidance → More problems → More shame → Repeat

Reset Spiral: Mistake → Self-compassion → Small action → Reconnection → Learning → Growth

Same starting point. Completely different destination.

The choice between these two spirals happens in the **first 60 seconds** after you realize you've made a mistake.

Common Shame Triggers and Reset Responses

Trigger: "I overspent again" **Shame Response:** "I have no self-control. I'll never change." **Reset Response:** "I was stressed and used an old coping mechanism. What do I need right now besides spending?"

Trigger: "I forgot to pay that bill" **Shame Response:** "I'm so irresponsible. I can't handle basic adulting." **Reset Response:** "My brain struggles with time management. Let me set up a system to catch this next time."

Trigger: "I avoided my finances for two weeks" **Shame Response:** "I'm pathetic. Everyone else can handle this." **Reset Response:** "Avoidance is a sign I was overwhelmed. Let me start with one small reconnection."

The reset response acknowledges the reality without attacking your character.

Breaking Shame in Real Time

Here's what it looks like when you catch shame in the moment:

1. **Feel the shame rising** ("Oh no, I did it again...")

2. **Pause and breathe** (literally stop what you're doing)

3. **Name it:** "I'm feeling shame about this money mistake"

4. **Interrupt:** "This feeling is temporary. The mistake doesn't define me."

5. **Take one tiny action** (check balance, write one note, move $1)

6. **Acknowledge yourself:** "I'm practicing coming back instead of hiding"

This process takes 2-3 minutes. But it can save you from weeks of avoidance.

When Shame Comes from Others

Sometimes shame doesn't just come from inside. Others might criticize your financial choices or ADHD-related struggles.

If someone says: "You just need more self-discipline." **You can think:** "They don't understand how ADHD affects financial management. I'm building systems that work for my brain."

If someone says: "You're being irresponsible." **You can think:** "I'm learning to be responsible in ways that actually work for me."

If someone says: "Just try harder." **You can think:** "I'm trying smarter, not harder."

You don't have to defend yourself out loud. But **you can defend yourself internally.**

Building Shame Resistance Over Time

The more you practice the shame reset, the less power shame has over you. You build:

Emotional Flexibility: You can feel shame without being controlled by it **Self-Compassion:** You treat yourself like a good friend **Growth Mindset:** Mistakes become learning opportunities **Resilience:** You bounce back faster each time

This isn't about eliminating shame completely. It's about **changing your relationship with it.**

Key Takeaway

You don't need to be perfect to reset. You just need to interrupt the shame before it becomes your story.

What to Do Next

1. Think of the last financial mistake that triggered shame

2. Write down the shame story your brain told you

3. Rewrite it as a reset story with self-compassion

4. Practice your shame interrupt phrase out loud

5. Take **one small action** to return to your financial system:

    - Open your account

    - Move $5

    - Update your dashboard

    - Write yourself an encouraging note

You are not your last mistake. You are your next reset. And you're doing it—right now.

Remember: **Shame is the voice of your past. Reset is the voice of your future.**

Which voice will you listen to today?

Chapter 14: Track Micro-Win Streak

Let Progress Be Your Dopamine Source

For most of my life, I thought you had to make *big* moves to make financial progress.

Save $1,000. Pay off an entire credit card. Stick to a budget for 30 days without a single mistake.

So I kept waiting for those "big win" moments. But they rarely came.

And while I waited, I ignored all the **small wins**—the ones that were already happening:

- Saying no to something I couldn't afford

- Tracking one transaction

- Canceling a forgotten subscription

- Logging into my account even when I didn't want to

- Moving $5 to savings—even if I moved it back later

I didn't recognize those moments as progress. Until I realized they weren't just wins—they were **streak-builders.**

Once I started tracking them, my brain changed. My money mindset changed. And my *identity* started to shift from "I'm bad with money" to *"I'm someone who makes progress every day."*

Why Micro-Wins Matter More Than Master Plans

When you live with ADHD, big plans can feel crushing. Because:

- They often require long-term consistency (which we struggle with)

- They delay rewards (which our brains crave now)

- They demand perfection (which leads to avoidance)

But micro-wins are different. They're:

- Small

- Instant

- Visible

- Encouraging

- Emotionally satisfying

- **Neurologically rewarding**

Each time you complete a micro-win, your brain gets a **dopamine hit**. That's the same brain chemical involved in motivation, memory, and momentum.

In other words: **you train yourself to keep showing up.**

Real Story: Maya's Win Tracker Shift

Maya was a 40-year-old graphic designer who hated budgeting. She tried every app. Every spreadsheet. Every envelope system. Nothing stuck.

But she loved sticker charts as a kid—so we created one for her finances.

Each day she:

- Tracked one transaction
- Did one reset
- Opened her account
- Or canceled one expense

She gave herself a sticker or checkmark for each win.

After 10 days, something shifted. "I'm not budgeting. I'm streaking," she said. "And I don't want to break it."

That's the psychology of micro-wins. They reframe your identity—not as a fixer, but as a builder.

How to Create a Micro-Win Streak (In 3 Steps)

Step 1: Define What a Win Looks Like for You

This isn't about perfection—it's about participation.

Here are some great micro-wins:

- Track one expense
- Cancel one subscription
- Move $1 to savings
- Say no to an impulse buy
- Do your weekly money reset
- Open your bank app
- Log a money win
- Set up one automation
- Read one chapter of this book
- Celebrate a boundary you held

Choose **3-5 actions** that feel doable and clear.

Step 2: Choose a Simple Tracker Format

Options:

- Notebook with daily checkboxes

- Google Sheet or digital habit tracker

- Bullet journal habit grid

- A wall calendar with stickers or stars

- Notes app list you update daily

What matters is **visibility**. Your brain needs to *see* the wins stack up.

Step 3: Set a Streak Goal

Start with something simple:

- 5 days in a row

- 10 wins in 14 days

- 15 checkmarks in 21 days

Make it flexible. This isn't a punishment system.

The goal isn't "never break the streak." It's to see your progress over time—and to feel the *identity shift* as it happens.

Why This Works (Even When You "Fall Off")

Streaks aren't about being perfect. They're about building **a new default identity**: *"I'm someone who stays connected to my money—even if I miss a day."*

If you break your streak?

- Don't throw away the whole system

- Just write: "Reset. Still showing up."

- And start again

This approach builds:

- Self-trust

- Emotional resilience

- A pattern of return—not perfection

That's what keeps momentum alive.

My Personal Micro-Win Ritual

I keep a monthly habit tracker with three money-related rows:

- Track a transaction

- Log a win

- Take one reset action

Each checkmark is a vote for my future self. And when I see the streaks build? It's not about the money. It's about who I'm becoming.

Key Takeaway

Small wins create safety. Streaks build belief. You're not behind—you're already in motion.

What to Do Next

1. Choose 3 simple micro-win actions

2. Create a visual tracker (paper, app, whiteboard—whatever works)

3. Set a streak goal (5 days? 10 wins in 2 weeks?)

4. Track daily or weekly

5. Celebrate—even if the action was small

Let your streak become your system. Let the system build your identity. And let your identity pull you into the future you've been afraid to believe in—until now.

Chapter 15: Create a One-Page Financial Dashboard

See Everything. Feel Less Overwhelmed. Take Back Control.

There was a time when I had financial data spread across five different apps, two notebooks, three bank accounts, and whatever was bouncing around in my head.

It wasn't a system. It was chaos disguised as "trying."

I'd toggle between apps to check balances. Scroll through emails for bills I forgot about. Avoid budgeting altogether because I couldn't even figure out where to begin.

The result? I felt like I was always behind—no matter how much progress I was actually making.

What I needed wasn't more tracking. What I needed was **visibility.** One page. One place. One calming glance.

That's when I created my first **financial dashboard**. And it changed everything.

Why Dashboards Work for ADHD Brains

We don't just need reminders. We need **anchors.**

Because ADHD makes it hard to:

- Hold multiple pieces of information at once

- Maintain financial object permanence

- Follow long-term plans without visual cues

- Remember where everything lives

- Stay emotionally regulated while facing our finances

A dashboard works because it:

- Makes everything visible at once

- Reduces the emotional effort of decision-making

- Simplifies priorities

- Gives your brain a "home base" to return to when you feel lost

It's not a spreadsheet. It's a map. And maps make journeys feel doable.

Real Story: Jordan's Dashboard Reset

Jordan was a self-employed ADHD coach with great income—but total financial overwhelm.

"I don't even know what I have," he said. "I'm making money. I just feel lost."

We built a one-page dashboard on paper. That's it.

It showed:

- What he had
- What he owed
- What he wanted to do next

After one week of using it, he said: "This page makes me feel like I can breathe again."

That's the point. **Clarity is calming.**

What to Include in Your Dashboard

This is not a budgeting tool. This is a **snapshot**—a calming overview of your financial life.

Pick and choose what feels most helpful.

Core Sections:

1. **Current Account Balances**

- Checking, savings, cash on hand

- Credit card balances

- Investment accounts (optional)

2. **Monthly Essentials**

   - Rent/mortgage

   - Utilities

   - Groceries

   - Minimum payments due

3. **Upcoming Payments**

   - Any known charges in the next 1-2 weeks

   - Subscriptions, bills, renewals

4. **Micro-Win Tracker**

   - Track small actions: money moved, resets done, subscriptions canceled

5. **Current Financial Focus**

   - What's the *one* thing you're working on right now? *(E.g., Build $500 buffer, track 5 expenses, cancel 3 subs)*

6. **Notes or Reflections**

   - "How did money feel this week?"

- "One win I'm proud of is..."

- "One thing to watch next week..."

This page is not here to judge you. It's here to **center you**.

How to Build It (Low-Tech or High-Tech)

You don't need a fancy tool. Try one of these:

- A physical page in your journal or planner

- A printable worksheet (you can even draw your own)

- A Google Doc or Notion template

- A whiteboard on your wall

- A dry erase sheet on your fridge

Whatever format works best, **keep it visible.** Because out of sight = out of mind = back to chaos.

Make It ADHD-Proof

A few design guidelines:

- Keep it to **one page**

- Use large, clear boxes or sections

- Use color to highlight categories

- Include blank space so it doesn't feel crowded

- Make it fun—name your goals, add stickers, write affirmations

Optional: Include reset rituals directly on the dashboard. This turns your tool into a **daily or weekly anchor**.

Why This Builds Confidence

When you create your own dashboard, you're:

- Taking control of the narrative

- Making your financial world smaller and more manageable

- Giving your brain an emotional reset point

- Reinforcing the identity: *"I am someone who sees the whole picture."*

You stop reacting. You start responding—with clarity.

My Dashboard Ritual

Every Sunday, I update my one-page dashboard. I write in balances. I check off micro wins. I write one sentence about how I feel about money that week. And I ask myself: "What's one thing I can move forward next?"

It's a five-minute ritual. But it reconnects me to everything that matters.

Key Takeaway

You don't need perfect systems. You just need a place to land. A dashboard gives you that place.

What to Do Next

1. Choose your format (paper, digital, journal, whiteboard)

2. Pick 3-5 categories to track (start small)

3. Create or draw your dashboard layout

4. Fill it in with what you know right now

5. Set a reminder to review and update it weekly

This is not about control. It's about calm. And it's one of the strongest ways to make your ADHD brain feel safe around money.

Chapter 16: Your New Money Identity

You're Not Just Changing Habits—You're Becoming Someone New

At the beginning of my money reset journey, I didn't believe I was someone who could "be good with money."

I believed I was the kind of person who:

- Always forgot due dates

- Spent emotionally when things got hard

- Made decent money but had nothing to show for it

- Would eventually "figure it out," but never quite did

I had evidence to back those stories up. But they weren't the truth. They were just **old identities**, reinforced by years of overwhelm, shame, and survival-mode decisions.

Here's what no one tells you when you're trying to get your money life together: **Changing your finances**

starts with changing the story you tell yourself about who you are.

Because behavior follows identity.

If you think you're someone who always messes up? You'll act like it. If you believe you're someone who always resets? You'll return, over and over, until the new path becomes who you are.

This final chapter is about closing the loop. Not just on your habits—but on your *old self-concept*.

Why Identity Is the Foundation for ADHD Transformation

ADHD doesn't just affect attention. It affects **self-perception**.

- We internalize years of missed deadlines, impulsive choices, and "not enoughs"

- We assume our mistakes mean something about our *worth*

- We carry emotional residue from every financial spiral we've ever had

- And we build a money identity around avoidance and failure—not action and growth

The result? We stay stuck in "fixing" mode.

But you don't need to fix yourself. You need to **see yourself differently.**

And every 5-minute reset you've done in this book has been a vote for that new version of you.

Real Story: Lani's Identity Shift

Lani was a 33-year-old creative who avoided money for most of her adult life.

She didn't think she was "bad with money." She thought she was *broken* with it.

Every time she tried to budget or save, she sabotaged herself. Not because she didn't care. Because deep down, she didn't believe she could become someone who *had control*.

Through this reset process, she started to tell a new story.

It didn't happen overnight. But the more she showed up—tracking one transaction, celebrating one win, resetting after one mess-up—the more she saw a different version of herself emerging.

She started using phrases like: "I'm learning how to be present with my money." "I'm rebuilding trust with myself." "I don't have to be perfect. I just have to return."

And when she reached $1,000 in her buffer fund, she didn't say "I finally saved something."

She said: *"I'm a saver now."*

That's identity. And it's everything.

Who Are You Becoming?

You're not the same person who picked up this book. You've already done the work to:

- Show up

- Reset

- Celebrate small wins

- Track progress

- Handle mess-ups

- Break shame loops

- Reframe avoidance as curiosity

So let's name your new identity—out loud.

Here's a prompt to finish:

"I used to believe I was someone who _____.
Now I'm becoming someone who _____."

Examples:

- "I used to believe I avoided money because I was weak. Now I'm becoming someone who faces my finances with clarity."

- "I used to see myself as an impulsive spender. Now I'm becoming a conscious decision-maker."

- "I used to fear the numbers. Now I log in without panic."

- "I used to disappear when things got hard. Now I return."

You don't have to be perfect. You just have to *believe* that showing up makes you someone new. Because it does.

Build an Identity That Sticks

Let's root your transformation in something concrete.

Create a New Identity Statement:

Use this formula: "I am someone who _____, even when _____."

Examples:

- "I am someone who resets, even when I mess up."

- "I am someone who checks in weekly, even when I feel behind."

- "I am someone who celebrates progress, even when it's small."

- "I am someone who stays connected to money, even when it's hard."

Write yours down. Post it. Speak it. Let it become your new baseline.

My Money Identity Mantra

Here's mine, the one I still use: "I'm not someone who gets it perfect. I'm someone who always comes back."

That one sentence rewrote years of financial shame. It gave me permission to grow. It gave me language that my nervous system could trust.

Now it's yours to rewrite.

Key Takeaway

You don't have to become someone else. You just have to return to the version of you that resets, rebuilds, and believes again.

What to Do Next

1. Write your "I used to... / now I..." identity shift

2. Create a money mantra that supports your reset journey

3. Post it where you'll see it during tough days

4. Speak it aloud every time you doubt your progress

Because this journey isn't about budgeting harder. It's about becoming someone who **keeps coming back**.

You already are.

Section 4:
ADVANCED RESILIENCE AND SUPPORT

Navigate crises, difficult conversations, and build lasting support systems.

Chapter 17: The Emergency Reset Plan

What to Do When Everything Falls Apart

Six months into my reset journey, I got blindsided.

My freelance client didn't pay a major invoice. My car needed $800 in repairs. And my laptop—my main work tool—decided to die on the same week.

Suddenly, all my careful resets felt pointless. I was back in crisis mode, making desperate decisions, avoiding my bank account, and spiraling into the old familiar panic.

I remember thinking: *"All that progress, and I'm right back where I started."*

But here's what I discovered: **Having an emergency reset plan isn't about preventing crisis. It's about knowing how to navigate crisis without losing yourself in it.**

This chapter is your emergency kit—the reset plan for when life hits hard and your financial world feels like it's crumbling.

Why ADHD Brains Need Crisis Plans

When everything goes wrong at once, ADHD brains don't just struggle financially—we struggle neurologically.

Crisis triggers:

- **Executive function shutdown** (we can't think clearly or prioritize)

- **Emotional flooding** (panic overrides logic)

- **Time collapse** (everything feels urgent right now)

- **Decision paralysis** (too many problems, can't pick where to start)

- **Shame spirals** ("I should have been more prepared")

Without a plan, we make reactive decisions that often make things worse. We avoid, we overspend on credit, we borrow from people we shouldn't, or we freeze completely.

But with an emergency reset plan? **You have a roadmap when your brain can't make one.**

My Crisis Wake-Up Call

That terrible week taught me something crucial: I had built great habits for normal times, but I had no system for abnormal times.

So I created what I call my **Emergency Reset Plan**—a simple, step-by-step guide I could follow when my brain was too overwhelmed to think clearly.

I've used it three times since then. Each time, it kept me from spiraling into the old patterns of avoidance and panic spending.

Here's how to build yours.

The 24-Hour Emergency Reset Protocol

When crisis hits, you have 24 hours to reset your relationship with the situation before panic takes over completely.

Hour 1: STOP and ASSESS

Before you do anything financial, reset your nervous system:

- Take 5 deep breaths

- Write down: "This is temporary. I will figure this out."

- List what actually happened (facts only, no stories)

Example: "Car repair: $800. Client payment delayed 2 weeks. Laptop died: $600 replacement needed."

Hours 2-3: TRIAGE

Not everything is equally urgent. Categorize your crisis:

- **Red (Handle today):** Overdrafts, bounced checks, immediate safety needs

- **Yellow (Handle this week):** Bills due soon, urgent repairs

- **Green (Handle this month):** Everything else

Focus only on Red items for now.

Hours 4-24: EMERGENCY MINI-RESETS

Pick ONE action from each category:

Immediate Relief:

- Call one creditor to explain and request extension

- Transfer any available money to cover Red items

- Cancel one non-essential expense to free up cash

Communication:

- Text one trusted person: "Having a financial crisis, but I'm handling it"

- Email delayed client with specific follow-up date

- Set phone reminder to revisit Yellow items tomorrow

Self-Care:

- Do your normal weekly money reset (even if numbers are scary)

- Write one thing you're grateful for

- Plan one small treat that costs nothing

The 30-Day Crisis Management Plan

After your 24-hour reset, you need a sustainable plan for the next month.

Week 1: Stabilize

- Focus only on Red and Yellow items

- Track every expense (crisis spending gets out of hand fast)

- Communicate with anyone you owe money to

- Ask for help from one trusted person

Week 2: Recalibrate

- Update your dashboard with new reality

- Identify which normal expenses you can pause

- Look for quick income opportunities

- Restart your micro-win streak (even tiny wins count)

Week 3: Rebuild

- Create a plan for Green items

- Start building crisis fund for next time

- Return to normal reset rituals

- Celebrate progress, however small

Week 4: Strengthen

- Reflect on what worked and what didn't

- Update your emergency plan based on what you learned

- Build one new financial buffer

- Acknowledge your resilience

Real Story: Carmen's Medical Crisis

Carmen, a 29-year-old teacher, ended up in the ER with appendicitis. Between the medical bills, missed work, and unexpected expenses, she was looking at $3,000 in costs she didn't have.

The 5-Minute Money Reset

Old Carmen would have panicked, avoided all financial tasks, and charged everything to credit cards.

Reset Carmen used her emergency plan:

24-Hour Reset:

- She wrote down the facts: "$3K total, $800 due immediately"

- She called the hospital billing department and got on a payment plan

- She asked her sister for a $500 loan with specific repayment terms

30-Day Plan:

- Week 1: She picked up two tutoring clients for extra income

- Week 2: She paused her streaming services and eating out

- Week 3: She started a "medical buffer fund" with $10/week

- Week 4: She had covered the immediate costs and felt in control again

"The crisis still sucked," she told me. "But I didn't disappear from my financial life. I stayed present and dealt with it."

Your Emergency Reset Checklist

Create this list now, before you need it:

My Crisis Contacts:

- One trusted friend I can call for emotional support

- One person I could ask for a small loan if absolutely necessary

- Financial institutions' customer service numbers

- One financial advisor or counselor (even if free)

My Crisis Actions:

- First place I'll look for emergency money

- First expense I'll cut if I need cash immediately

- My "minimum viable" monthly budget for crisis mode

- One side income I could start quickly

My Crisis Mantras:

- "This is temporary. I will figure this out."

- "I don't have to solve everything today."

- "Asking for help is a sign of strength, not weakness."

- "I've handled hard things before. I can handle this."

Building Your Crisis Buffer

You don't need a full emergency fund to start. You need a **crisis starter fund**—even $100 makes a difference when you're panicking.

Build it through:

- $5/week automatic transfer

- All found money (returns, refunds, gift cards)

- 50% of any unexpected income

- Money from subscriptions you cancel

The goal isn't perfection. It's **creating a small buffer between you and complete panic.**

Why This Approach Works

Traditional emergency advice says "save 3-6 months of expenses." For ADHD brains in crisis, that feels impossible and unhelpful.

This approach works because:

- It's designed for overwhelmed brains

- It focuses on immediate action, not perfect planning

- It builds on the reset skills you already have

- It treats crisis as a temporary state, not a permanent failure

Most importantly: **It keeps you connected to your financial life instead of fleeing from it.**

My Current Emergency Plan

I keep a one-page emergency plan in my phone notes. It has:

- My crisis checklist

- Three people I can call

- My minimum monthly budget

- Reminder of my strongest financial skills

I review it every few months and update it based on life changes.

I hope I never need it again. But if I do? **I won't be starting from panic. I'll be starting from a plan.**

Key Takeaway

Crisis doesn't erase your progress. It tests your foundation. And you're stronger than you think.

What to Do Next

1. Create your emergency reset checklist (even if you don't need it now)

2. Start a crisis buffer with $5 this week

3. Identify one person you could ask for support

4. Write your crisis mantras somewhere you can find them

5. Remember: You're not planning for failure—you're planning for resilience

Because the goal isn't to avoid every crisis.

The goal is to stay yourself through every crisis.

Chapter 18: Money Conversations That Don't End in Meltdowns

How to Talk About Finances Without Losing Your Mind

"We need to talk about money."

Those six words used to make my stomach drop and my brain fog roll in like a storm. Whether it was with a partner, parent, roommate, or financial advisor—money conversations felt like emotional minefields.

I'd either shut down completely, get defensive, or agree to things I didn't understand just to end the conversation faster. Then I'd walk away feeling confused, resentful, and more disconnected from my finances than before.

Sound familiar?

For ADHD brains, money conversations aren't just challenging—they can be neurologically overwhelming. But they're also unavoidable. And when handled right, they can actually strengthen your financial confidence instead of destroying it.

This chapter is your guide to having money conversations that don't end in meltdowns, shutdowns, or resentments.

Why Money Conversations Trigger ADHD Brains

It's not just you. There are real neurological reasons why financial discussions feel so hard:

Emotional Flooding: Money topics trigger our amygdala (fear center) faster than our prefrontal cortex (logic center) can respond.

Processing Speed: We need more time to process complex information, but conversations move in real-time.

Rejection Sensitivity: We're hyperaware of criticism or judgment, so we interpret questions as attacks.

Working Memory: We struggle to hold multiple financial concepts in our heads while formulating responses.

Time Pressure: Conversations feel urgent even when they're not, triggering our panic response.

Understanding this isn't making excuses—it's **making strategies.**

The Conversation That Changed Everything

Two years into my reset journey, my partner asked if we could "discuss our financial goals."

Old me would have panicked. But reset me had been practicing. I said: "Yes, but can we do it differently this time?"

Instead of diving in immediately, I asked for:

- 24 hours to prepare my thoughts

- A written agenda so I knew what to expect

- Permission to take breaks if I got overwhelmed

- A recap email afterward to confirm what we decided

That conversation went better than any money talk I'd ever had. Not because we agreed on everything, but because **I stayed present for the whole thing.**

That's when I realized: The problem wasn't the money. It was the conversation structure.

The ADHD-Friendly Money Conversation Framework

Use this framework whether you're talking with partners, family, financial advisors, or even yourself.

BEFORE the Conversation:

Set the Container

- Choose timing when you're not tired or stressed

- Pick a neutral location (not the bedroom or kitchen table where you pay bills)

- Set a time limit (30-45 minutes max for ADHD brains)

- Agree on the specific topic (not "let's talk about money"—too vague)

Prepare Your Brain

- Write down your main concerns beforehand

- List questions you want to ask

- Note any triggers or sensitive areas

- Remind yourself: "This person is not my enemy"

DURING the Conversation:

Use the PAUSE Method

P - Pause when you feel flooded ("Can we pause for a second?") **A** - Acknowledge what you heard ("So you're saying...") **U** - Understand before responding ("Help me understand why...") **S** - Speak your truth calmly ("My perspective is...") **E** - End with next steps ("So we'll both...")

Ask for What You Need

- "Can you repeat that last part?"

- "I need a minute to process this"

- "Can we slow down a bit?"

- "Let me write that down so I don't forget"

AFTER the Conversation:

Integration Time

- Take 15 minutes alone to decompress

- Write down key points while they're fresh

- Note any follow-up actions

- Celebrate that you stayed engaged

Real Conversation Scripts

Here are actual phrases that have saved me from money conversation meltdowns:

When You Need Processing Time:

- "This is important to me, so I want to think about it carefully. Can I get back to you tomorrow?"

- "I'm feeling a bit overwhelmed. Can we take a 5-minute break?"

- "I want to make sure I understand. Can you help me recap what we've covered?"

When You Disagree:

- "I see it differently. Can I share my perspective?"

- "I understand your point. I'm concerned about..."

- "What if we tried it for one month and then reevaluated?"

When You Don't Understand:

- "I want to make sure I get this right. Can you explain it differently?"

- "Can you give me an example of how that would work?"

- "I need to research this more before I can decide."

When You Feel Judged:

- "I'm feeling defensive right now. Can we approach this differently?"

- "I know my money habits haven't been perfect. I'm working on improving them."

- "I'm doing the best I can with the tools I have right now."

The "Financial Meeting" Approach

For ongoing relationships (partners, family, financial advisors), consider creating regular "financial meetings" instead of random money conversations.

Monthly Partner Money Meetings:

- Same time each month (like the last Sunday)
- Clear agenda sent 24 hours ahead
- 30-minute time limit
- Celebrate wins first, then address challenges
- End with one action item each

Quarterly Family Money Check-ins:

- Review shared goals and expenses
- Discuss any changes needed
- Plan for upcoming major expenses
- Keep it factual, not emotional

This approach removes the surprise element that often triggers ADHD overwhelm.

When Someone Else Brings Up Money Unexpectedly

Sometimes you can't control when money conversations happen. Here's your emergency protocol:

Buy Yourself Time:

- "This is important. Can we schedule time to talk about it properly?"

- "I want to give this the attention it deserves. How about tomorrow evening?"

- "Let me grab a pen so I can take notes."

If You Must Talk Now:

- Ask them to slow down

- Repeat back what you understand

- Focus on understanding, not solving

- Agree only to have another conversation, not to final decisions

If You Start to Flood:

- "I'm getting overwhelmed. Can we pause?"

- "I need a bathroom break" (gives you 5 minutes to reset)

- "This is a lot to process. Let me think about it."

Dealing with Judgment and Criticism

Money conversations often come with judgment, especially if your ADHD has created financial challenges. Here's how to handle it:

When Someone Says: "You just need to be more responsible." **You Can Say:** "I'm working on systems that work better for how my brain processes information."

When Someone Says: "Why can't you just make a budget and stick to it?" **You Can Say:** "I've tried traditional budgeting. I'm finding approaches that work better for me."

When Someone Says: "You're being too sensitive about money." **You Can Say:** "Money feels big to me right now. I'm learning to approach it more calmly."

The goal isn't to educate them about ADHD (unless you want to). **The goal is to protect your emotional energy while staying engaged.**

Building Your Money Conversation Confidence

Like anything else, this gets easier with practice. Start small:

- Practice having money conversations with yourself out loud

- Try one money topic with your most supportive friend

- Join online ADHD financial support groups to practice virtually

- Work with an ADHD-friendly financial advisor or coach

Each positive money conversation builds evidence that **you can handle these discussions without falling apart.**

My Money Conversation Rules

These are the boundaries I've set for myself:

1. **No major financial decisions during emotional conversations**

2. **I can ask for time to think about anything**

3. **I can request written follow-up for complex topics**

4. **I will not be shamed for my ADHD-related money challenges**

5. **I am allowed to advocate for conversation structures that work for me**

These rules have saved me from agreeing to things I didn't understand or couldn't follow through on.

Key Takeaway

Money conversations don't have to be emotional disasters. With the right structure and boundaries, they can actually build financial confidence.

What to Do Next

1. Identify one money conversation you've been avoiding

2. Use the BEFORE framework to prepare for it

3. Practice one script from this chapter out loud

4. Set one boundary around how you want money conversations to go

5. Schedule a practice conversation with someone supportive

Remember: **You don't have to be perfect at money conversations. You just have to be present for them.**

And presence, like everything else in this book, is a skill you can develop—one conversation at a time.

Chapter 19: Building Your Money Support System

You Don't Have to Do This Alone

For the longest time, I thought managing money was supposed to be a solo activity.

I believed that asking for help meant I was failing. That needing support proved I was "bad with money." That if I were truly responsible, I'd figure it all out by myself.

So I struggled in isolation. I made the same mistakes over and over. I reinvented wheels that others had already perfected. And I stayed stuck longer than I needed to because I was too proud—or too ashamed—to ask for guidance.

Here's what I wish someone had told me years ago: **The most financially successful people aren't the ones who do everything themselves. They're the ones who build strong support systems.**

This final practical chapter is about creating your money support network—the people, resources, and structures that will help you maintain your resets long after you close this book.

Why ADHD Brains Need Extra Support

Traditional financial advice assumes you can maintain motivation, remember systems, and stay consistent through willpower alone. But ADHD brains benefit enormously from external support because:

External Accountability: We do better with outside structure than internal discipline **Pattern Recognition:** Others can spot our blind spots and recurring patterns **Emotional Regulation:** Having support reduces the shame that derails progress **Executive Function Backup:** When our brains are overloaded, others can help us think clearly **Celebration Amplification:** Sharing wins makes them feel more real and motivating

This isn't weakness. **It's strategy.**

The Five Types of Money Support

Not all support is created equal. You need different people for different purposes:

1. The Accountability Partner - Someone who checks in on your progress without judgment **2. The Practical Helper** - Someone who helps with actual tasks when you're overwhelmed **3. The Emotional Support** - Someone who listens without trying to fix everything **4. The Knowledge Source** - Someone who knows more than you and can teach/guide **5. The Celebration Witness** - Someone who gets genuinely excited about your wins

You don't need five different people—some can wear multiple hats. But **you do need each type of support.**

Real Story: How Maya Built Her Money Team

Maya realized she was trying to handle everything alone and burning out every few months. Here's the support team she assembled:

Accountability Partner: Her sister texts her every Sunday: "Did you do your money reset this week?"

Practical Helper: Her girlfriend helps her organize receipts once a month when Maya's ADHD makes it overwhelming.

Emotional Support: Her therapist, who understands both ADHD and financial anxiety.

Knowledge Source: An ADHD-friendly financial advisor she meets with quarterly.

Celebration Witness: Her best friend, who genuinely celebrates every financial milestone, no matter how small.

"I thought asking for help meant I was failing," Maya said. "Turns out, asking for help is what finally made me successful."

How to Find Your Support People

Start with Your Existing Network

Look for people who:

- Don't judge your ADHD struggles

- Celebrate your wins genuinely

- Can be trusted with sensitive information

- Have complementary strengths to your challenges

Be Specific About What You Need

Instead of: "Can you help me with money?" Try: "Would you be willing to text me once a week to ask if I've checked my bank account?"

Instead of: "I'm bad with money." Try: "I'm building better financial habits. Could I share my wins with you?"

Professional Support Options

- **ADHD-informed financial advisors** (search "fee-only financial planners" + "ADHD")

- **Financial therapists** (combine money skills with emotional support)

- **ADHD coaches** who include financial goals

- **Online ADHD financial communities** (Reddit, Facebook groups, Discord servers)

- **Body doubling services** for financial tasks

The Support Request Scripts

Asking for help feels vulnerable. Here are scripts that work:

For Accountability: "I'm working on better financial habits. Would you be willing to check in with me once a week? I'm not asking you to manage my money—just ask if I did my weekly money check-in."

For Practical Help: "I have ADHD and sometimes organizing financial paperwork gets overwhelming. Would you be willing to sit with me once a month while I sort through receipts? I'll provide the snacks."

For Emotional Support: "I'm learning to have a healthier relationship with money, but it brings up anxiety sometimes. Would you be someone I could text when I'm feeling overwhelmed about finances?"

For Knowledge: "You seem to have a good handle on your finances. Could I ask you a few questions about [specific topic]? I'm not asking you to be my financial advisor—just looking for some practical perspective."

Setting Boundaries with Money Support

Good support requires clear boundaries:

What You Will Share:

- Your goals and progress

- Specific questions or challenges

- Wins you want to celebrate

What You Won't Share:

- Exact account balances (unless relevant)

- Every financial detail

- Decisions that aren't their business

What You'll Ask For:

- Specific types of help

- Time-limited support

- Non-judgmental listening

What You Won't Ask For:

- Money (unless it's an emergency and you've agreed to this beforehand)

- Them to manage your finances

- Unlimited emotional labor

Creating Reciprocal Support

The best support relationships benefit both people. Consider:

- **Skill trading:** You help with their ADHD challenges, they help with financial organization

- **Mutual accountability:** You both check in on each other's goals

- **Information sharing:** You both research and share helpful resources

- **Celebration partnerships:** You both share wins and provide encouragement

When Support Isn't Working

Sometimes support relationships need adjustment:

If someone is too judgmental: "I appreciate your concern, but I need support that doesn't include criticism of my past decisions."

If someone tries to take over: "Thank you for wanting to help. Right now I need encouragement more than solutions."

If someone isn't reliable: Find additional support sources rather than relying on one person.

If you feel like a burden: Remember that most people genuinely want to help and feel good when they can contribute to your success.

Digital Support Tools

Technology can provide consistent support when humans aren't available:

Apps for Accountability:

- ADHD financial communities

- Body doubling platforms

- Progress tracking apps

- Reminder systems

Professional Support:

- Online ADHD financial coaches

- Virtual financial therapy

- ADHD-friendly budgeting services

- Telehealth for financial anxiety

My Personal Support System

Here's how my support looks today:

Accountability: My partner asks about my weekly money reset **Practical:** My ADHD coach helps me troubleshoot system breakdowns **Emotional:** My therapy specifically addresses money anxiety **Knowledge:** My financial advisor understands ADHD challenges **Celebration:** My sister gets genuinely excited about every financial milestone

This took time to build. Start with one person and one type of support.

Building Support for Different Life Stages

Your support needs will evolve:

Early Recovery: Focus on emotional support and accountability **Building Momentum:** Add knowledge sources and practical helpers **Maintaining Success:** Emphasize celebration witnesses and peer support **Major Life Changes:** Temporarily increase all types of support

The Support You Give Yourself

External support amplifies internal support. Keep developing:

- **Self-compassion** when you make mistakes
- **Self-celebration** when you succeed
- **Self-advocacy** when asking for what you need
- **Self-trust** that you can handle challenges

You are your own most important support person.

Creating a Support Plan

Write down:

1. **What types of support do I need most right now?**

2. **Who in my current network might be able to provide each type?**

3. **What specific request could I make to each person?**

4. **What professional support might benefit me?**

5. **How can I reciprocate or contribute to others?**

Start with one request to one person this week.

Key Takeaway

Financial independence doesn't mean doing everything alone. It means building systems and relationships that support your success.

What to Do Next

1. Identify one type of support you need most

2. Think of one person who might be able to provide it

3. Use one of the scripts to make a specific request

4. Consider one form of professional support that appeals to you

5. Remember: Asking for help is a sign of wisdom, not weakness

Building a support system takes time and courage. But **you don't have to transform your financial life in isolation.**

The strongest financial foundation isn't built alone— it's built with others who understand your journey and want to see you succeed.

You've learned to reset your money. Now build the community that will help you keep resetting for years to come.

Chapter 20: ADHD-Proof Your Financial Future

Building Long-Term Wealth Without Losing Your Mind

For years, I thought "investing" and "long-term planning" were for people who had their financial lives completely figured out.

People who never forgot to pay bills. People who could stick to budgets for months at a time. People whose brains didn't shut down when faced with complex financial decisions.

In other words—not me.

I assumed I needed to master basic money management before I could even think about building wealth. So I kept putting it off, waiting for the day I'd become the kind of person who could handle "advanced" financial strategies.

That day never came. Because I was thinking about it all wrong.

Here's what I discovered: **ADHD brains can be excellent at building long-term wealth—but only when we use approaches designed for how we actually think and function.**

This chapter is about setting up your financial future in ways that work with your ADHD brain, not against it.

Why Traditional Investing Advice Fails ADHD Brains

Most investment guidance assumes you can:

- Research investments thoroughly before deciding

- Monitor your portfolio regularly without obsessing

- Stick to a strategy through market ups and downs

- Remember to increase contributions annually

- Balance multiple complex financial goals simultaneously

But ADHD brains often experience:

- **Analysis paralysis** when faced with too many investment options

- **Hyper-focus periods** followed by complete avoidance

- **Emotional reactivity** to market fluctuations

- **Time blindness** that makes long-term planning feel abstract

- **Working memory issues** that make complex strategies hard to follow

The solution isn't to avoid investing. It's to **invest in ways that work with these tendencies.**

My Investing Wake-Up Call

Three years into my reset journey, I realized I'd gotten good at managing my day-to-day money but was still avoiding anything "investment-related."

I had built up a decent emergency fund, but it was just sitting in a regular savings account earning basically nothing. Meanwhile, I was watching friends talk about their retirement accounts and feeling that familiar ADHD shame: *"I should know this stuff by now."*

The breakthrough came when I stopped trying to become an investment expert and started applying reset principles to wealth building: **Start small, keep it simple, automate everything possible.**

My first investment was $25 a week into a target-date fund. That was it. No research paralysis. No complex strategies. Just $25 a week, automatically withdrawn, into the most boring investment possible.

That single automation has grown into the foundation of my financial security. Not because I became a brilliant investor, but because I made it **impossible to mess up.**

The ADHD Investing Philosophy

Forget everything you've heard about active investing, stock picking, or market timing. For ADHD brains, successful investing follows three simple principles:

1. Automate Everything If you have to remember to do it, you won't do it consistently.

2. Keep It Boring The more complex your strategy, the more likely you are to abandon it.

3. Start Stupidly Small It's better to invest $10 consistently than $500 sporadically.

That's it. Everything else is just details.

The 5-Minute Investment Setup

Here's how to start building wealth without overwhelming your ADHD brain:

Step 1: Open One Simple Account

Choose either:

- Your employer's 401(k) if they offer matching (free money)

- A Roth IRA at a low-cost provider (Fidelity, Vanguard, Schwab)

Don't research for weeks. Pick one and move on.

Step 2: Choose One Boring Investment

Select a target-date fund that matches roughly when you want to retire. For example:

- Planning to retire around 2055? Pick a "Target Date 2055" fund

- Don't overthink this. These funds automatically adjust as you age.

Step 3: Set Up Automatic Contributions

Start with an amount so small it feels almost embarrassing:

- $25 per week

- $50 per month

- Whatever feels easy and sustainable

Step 4: Forget About It

Seriously. Set a calendar reminder to check it once per year. That's it.

This approach removes all the decision points that typically derail ADHD financial progress.

Real Story: Marcus and the $20 Retirement Plan

Marcus, a 28-year-old software developer with ADHD, felt completely overwhelmed by retirement planning. He'd started and abandoned three different investment strategies in two years.

We applied the reset approach: He opened a Roth IRA and set up a $20 weekly automatic transfer into a target-date fund.

"Twenty dollars?" he said. "That seems pointless."

But $20 weekly turned into $1,040 in the first year. Then we gradually increased it to $30, then $50, then $75 as it became routine.

Three years later, he has over $8,000 invested and has never missed a contribution or changed his strategy. The key wasn't the amount—it was the **consistency enabled by simplicity.**

Building Wealth Through Reset Principles

Apply the same reset thinking to long-term wealth building:

Micro-Actions Build Macro Results

- $25/week for 30 years at 7% growth = $325,000

- Small, consistent actions compound dramatically over time

Automate Your Future Self

- Set up increases to happen automatically each year

- Remove your present self from future financial decisions

Progress Over Perfection

- Starting late is better than never starting

- A simple plan you follow beats a perfect plan you abandon

Identity-Based Investing

- "I'm someone who invests for my future"

- "I'm building wealth slowly and steadily"

ADHD-Friendly Investment Rules

Rule 1: Never invest money you'll need within 5 years Keep emergency funds and short-term savings separate from investments.

Rule 2: Ignore daily market movements Check your accounts quarterly at most. Daily checking triggers emotional decisions.

Rule 3: Increase contributions, don't change strategies When you get raises or bonuses, increase contributions rather than complicating your approach.

Rule 4: Use target-date funds until you have $100,000+ Only consider more complex strategies once you have substantial assets.

Rule 5: Automate increases annually Set up 1-2% automatic increases each year so you don't have to remember.

What About Emergency Funds vs. Investing?

This is a common ADHD dilemma: Should I build my emergency fund first or start investing?

Here's the reset approach:

- Build a $1,000 mini emergency fund first

- Then split new savings: 50% to complete emergency fund, 50% to investing

- Once you have 3-6 months of expenses saved, focus primarily on investing

This prevents the all-or-nothing thinking that keeps many ADHD brains stuck.

Dealing with Investment Anxiety

ADHD brains often experience intense anxiety around investments because:

- We catastrophize market downturns

- We hyper-focus on daily losses

- We feel like we should "do something" when markets are volatile

Your anti-anxiety toolkit:

- Remember: You're investing for decades, not months

- Historical perspective: Markets always recover from downturns

- Automate everything so you can't make emotional decisions

- Focus on contributions, not account values

- Use the "sleep test": If your investment strategy keeps you awake at night, simplify it

Beyond Basic Investing: ADHD-Friendly Wealth Building

Once your basic investment routine is solid, consider these ADHD-friendly strategies:

Real Estate Through REITs

- Get real estate exposure without being a landlord

- Automatic, hands-off real estate investment

I Bonds for Inflation Protection

- Government bonds that adjust for inflation

- Can only buy $10,000 per year (built-in limitation prevents overthinking)

529 Plans for Kids' Education

- State tax benefits in many states

- Automate contributions and forget about them

Health Savings Accounts (HSAs)

- Triple tax advantage if you have a high-deductible health plan

- Becomes an additional retirement account after age 65

Setting Up Annual Investment Reviews

Instead of constant monitoring, schedule one annual "Investment Reset Day":

Your Annual Investment Reset Checklist:

- Review your contributions—can you increase them?

- Rebalance if necessary (most target-date funds do this automatically)

- Update beneficiaries if life circumstances changed

- Celebrate your progress, however small

- Set next year's contribution increase

Make this a celebration, not a chore. Order your favorite takeout, play good music, and acknowledge the progress you've made.

Building Wealth as an ADHD Entrepreneur

If you're self-employed or have variable income:

Set Up a SEP-IRA or Solo 401(k)

- Higher contribution limits than traditional IRAs

- Perfect for freelancers and business owners

Automate Based on Good Months

- When you have a big income month, automatically move a percentage to investments

- Don't wait for "regular" income to start building wealth

Separate Business and Personal Investing

- Keep business emergency funds separate from personal investments

- Don't invest money you might need for business expenses

My Current Investment Approach

Today, my investment strategy is embarrassingly simple:

- 401(k) with employer matching (automated)

- Roth IRA with target-date fund (automated)

- Taxable account with broad market index fund (automated)

- Annual review every December with celebratory dinner

Total time spent managing investments: About 2 hours per year.

This approach has built substantial wealth not through brilliance, but through **consistent automation that works with my ADHD brain.**

Key Takeaway

You don't need to be a financial genius to build wealth. You just need systems that work when your motivation doesn't.

What to Do Next

1. Choose one investment account to open (401(k) or Roth IRA)

2. Select one simple investment (target-date fund)

3. Set up automatic contributions (start small)

4. Schedule your first annual review for one year from now

5. Celebrate taking this step—you're now an investor

Remember: **The best investment strategy is the one you'll actually follow.** Keep it simple, keep it automated, and let time do the heavy lifting.

Your ADHD brain isn't a barrier to building wealth—it just needs the right approach.

Chapter 21: The Reset Lifestyle

Making Money Management Feel Natural,
Not Forced

Five years ago, managing money felt like wearing clothes that didn't fit. Every financial task was awkward, uncomfortable, and required enormous effort to maintain.

Today, my money resets feel as natural as brushing my teeth. Not because I've become a different person, but because I've built a **lifestyle** around the way my brain actually works.

The difference between having financial tools and living a financial lifestyle is the difference between surviving and thriving. Tools help you get through crises. Lifestyle helps you prevent them.

This final chapter is about making reset thinking so woven into your daily life that good financial choices become automatic—not through willpower, but through **design.**

What Is a Reset Lifestyle?

A reset lifestyle isn't about being perfect with money. It's about building a life where:

- Financial engagement feels natural, not forced

- Money mistakes trigger curiosity, not shame

- Your environment supports good financial choices

- Progress happens through rhythm, not intensity

- Money serves your values instead of controlling them

It's the difference between **doing** financial resets and **being** someone who resets.

How My Life Changed

Let me paint you a picture of how different my relationship with money feels now:

Old me:

- Avoided bank apps until forced to check

- Felt panic when unexpected expenses arose

- Made financial decisions reactively, often while stressed

- Believed money management required constant vigilance

- Felt guilty about every non-essential purchase

Reset lifestyle me:

- Check accounts weekly as part of my Sunday routine

- Have automated systems that handle most decisions

- Approach money choices with curiosity instead of anxiety

- Trust my systems to work even when I'm not thinking about money

- Spend on things I value without guilt because it's planned for

This transformation didn't happen overnight. It happened through thousands of tiny adjustments that eventually became a new way of living.

Building Your Financial Environment

Your environment shapes your choices more than your willpower ever could. Here's how to design surroundings that support reset thinking:

Physical Environment:

- Keep one notebook or folder for all financial documents

- Create a designated spot for receipts (bowl, envelope, app)

- Post your financial priorities somewhere visible

- Remove payment methods from shopping apps you use impulsively

- Keep cash in your wallet for small purchases that help you stay mindful

Digital Environment:

- Organize bank apps in one folder on your phone

- Set up automatic transfers so good choices happen without thinking

- Use calendar reminders for your weekly money reset

- Unsubscribe from retailer emails that trigger spending

- Follow social media accounts that support financial growth

Emotional Environment:

- Surround yourself with people who support your financial goals

- Practice talking about money in neutral, non-emotional terms

- Celebrate financial wins, no matter how small

- Create mantras or phrases that ground you during money stress

- Build regular rituals that keep you connected to your values

The Daily Reset Rhythms

Instead of thinking about money management as a separate activity, weave micro-resets throughout your regular routines:

Morning Ritual (30 seconds):

- Check your bank balance while drinking coffee
- Move any "found money" (refunds, cash back) to savings
- Set intention for mindful spending that day

Workday Rhythms:

- Track one purchase in real-time (receipt in designated spot)
- Use the spending reset ritual before any non-essential purchases
- Check in with your daily money intention during lunch break

Evening Wind-Down (2 minutes):

- Log the day's expenses (even just mentally reviewing)
- Move any loose change to savings jar

- Acknowledge one good financial choice you made

Weekend Deeper Connections:

- Sunday money reset ritual

- Update your financial dashboard

- Plan upcoming expenses and celebrations

These aren't rigid requirements—they're **opportunities to stay connected** without making money management feel like work.

Seasonal Financial Rhythms

Just like your energy and focus change with seasons, your financial attention can have natural rhythms:

Quarterly Deep Dives (4 times per year):

- Review and adjust automatic transfers

- Celebrate progress toward your chosen financial priority

- Check in with your support system

- Update your emergency reset plan

Annual Financial Retreat (once per year):

- Review your financial identity and goals

- Adjust investment contributions

- Organize tax documents

- Plan major expenses for the coming year

- Celebrate how far you've come

Monthly Maintenance:

- Update your dashboard

- Review and cancel any new subscription leaks

- Check progress on your current $100 challenge

- Connect with your accountability partner

This rhythm approach prevents the feast-or-famine cycle that exhausts ADHD brains.

Teaching Reset Principles to Others

One of the strongest signs that reset thinking has become lifestyle is when you naturally share these principles with others—family members, friends, especially ADHD kids who struggle with money concepts.

For ADHD Children:

- Start with physical money so they can see transactions

- Use clear jars for saving/spending/giving so progress is visible

- Create immediate rewards for saving milestones

- Practice the spending pause with small purchases

- Teach identity-based thinking: "I'm someone who saves for things I want"

For Partners and Family:

- Share your reset language and approaches

- Model self-compassion around money mistakes

- Create family financial rituals that feel positive

- Use your dashboard approach for household budgeting

- Demonstrate that money management can be calm and collaborative

For Friends and Community:

- Share wins and challenges without shame

- Offer support during their financial crises

- Recommend ADHD-friendly resources and approaches

- Normalize conversations about money and mental health

Handling Life Transitions Without Losing Your Reset

Life changes—new jobs, relationships, moves, health issues—can disrupt even the best financial rhythms. Here's how to maintain reset thinking through transitions:

Before Major Changes:

- Document your current systems so you can rebuild them quickly

- Identify which resets are most essential to maintain

- Build extra buffer in emergency funds

- Inform your support system about upcoming changes

During Transitions:

- Lower your expectations for financial complexity

- Focus on basic resets: track one transaction, weekly check-ins

- Use your emergency reset plan liberally

- Practice extra self-compassion around money mistakes

After Transitions:

- Gradually rebuild your fuller reset systems

- Update your dashboard and priorities based on new circumstances

- Celebrate maintaining any financial connection during chaotic times

- Learn from what worked and what didn't during the transition

Creating Your Personal Reset Legacy

Think about the financial story you want to tell in 10, 20, or 30 years. Not just about accumulating wealth, but about **how you want to relate to money** throughout your life.

Consider questions like:

- What do I want my relationship with money to model for others?

- How do I want to feel when I think about my financial choices?

- What kind of financial support do I want to be able to provide?

- How can my money reflect my deepest values?

- What financial legacy do I want to leave?

Your reset lifestyle should align with these deeper intentions, not just short-term financial goals.

Real Story: Elena's Family Reset Culture

Elena, a mother of two ADHD kids, realized that her financial resets were influencing her entire family's relationship with money.

Her 8-year-old started asking to "check our family money" during Sunday resets. Her teenager began using spending pause techniques before online purchases. Her partner adopted her micro-win tracking for his business expenses.

"I thought I was just fixing my own money problems," Elena said. "But I accidentally created a family culture where money isn't scary or shameful—it's just another thing we handle together."

This is the power of lifestyle change: it ripples outward, creating positive change beyond just your own financial situation.

Maintaining Long-Term Motivation

Reset lifestyle isn't about constant motivation—it's about building systems that work when motivation is low. But there are ways to nurture ongoing engagement:

Connect to Your Values:

- Regularly remind yourself why financial stability matters to you

- Link money goals to experiences and relationships you care about

- Practice gratitude for your progress, however small

Build in Variety:

- Rotate between different types of resets to prevent boredom

- Try new approaches occasionally while maintaining core systems

- Set new challenges when old ones become routine

Document Your Journey:

- Keep a simple journal of financial wins and lessons learned

- Take screenshots of milestones (account balances, debt payoffs)

- Write letters to your future self about current financial hopes

Celebrate Consistently:

- Acknowledge weekly wins, not just major milestones

- Share progress with your support system

- Treat yourself (within your reward budget) for consistency

The Compound Effect of Small Changes

After years of living with reset principles, I've seen how tiny daily choices compound into massive life changes:

- Five-minute weekly resets have created deep financial confidence

- $25 weekly investments have built substantial wealth

- Daily transaction tracking has eliminated financial blind spots

- Regular shame resets have healed decades of money anxiety

- Simple automation has prevented countless financial crises

None of these individual actions felt transformative at the time. But together, sustained over years, they've created a completely different financial reality.

What Reset Lifestyle Feels Like

When money management becomes lifestyle rather than task, you'll notice:

- **Financial decisions feel easier** because you have established rhythms and values to guide them

- **Money stress decreases significantly** because you trust your systems and your ability to handle challenges

- **You recover from setbacks faster** because you have practiced returning rather than avoiding

- **Money serves your life goals** instead of creating barriers to them

- **You feel proud of your progress** instead of ashamed of your imperfections

This isn't perfection—it's **sustainable excellence** designed for real life with an ADHD brain.

Your Reset Lifestyle Plan

As you finish this book, consider:

1. **Which resets felt most natural to you?** Build your lifestyle around these.

2. **What rhythms match your energy patterns?** Design your money management around your natural cycles.

3. **Who in your life can support this lifestyle?** Include them in your journey.

4. **What environment changes would make good choices easier?** Start with one physical change this week.

5. **How will you maintain connection to your values?** Build regular reminder practices.

Key Takeaway

A reset lifestyle isn't about managing money perfectly. It's about building a life where money management feels natural, supported, and aligned with who you're becoming.

What to Do Next

1. Choose one environmental change to support your financial goals

2. Design one daily micro-reset that fits naturally into your routine

3. Plan your first seasonal financial review

4. Share one reset principle with someone in your life

5. Write down what you want your financial lifestyle to look like in 5 years

The tools in this book will serve you well. But the lifestyle you build around them will serve you for life.

You're not just learning to reset your money. **You're learning to reset your entire relationship with**

financial security, abundance, and the role money plays in creating the life you actually want.

And that's a transformation that extends far beyond your bank account.

Conclusion and Final: You're Not Behind— You've Already Begun

The Real Transformation Happens in the Moments Between Resets

As I write this conclusion, I'm sitting at the same kitchen table where I once sat paralyzed, unable to open my banking app. The same place where shame used to live so loudly that I couldn't hear anything else.

But something fundamental has changed. Not just in my bank account—though that's improved too. The real change is in the story I tell myself when I sit down to face my money.

I no longer brace for impact. I no longer assume the worst. I no longer disappear when things get messy.

Instead, I reset. And that makes all the difference.

You didn't just read a book. You built a new relationship—with money, with progress, and most importantly, with yourself.

Every reset in these pages has been more than a tip or a technique. It's been a tool for identity change. And that's the real transformation: Not fixing your finances, but **resetting how you see yourself in the process.**

This Was Never About Perfect Budgets

When people ask me what this book is really about, I tell them it's not about money. It's about **coming home to yourself.**

For too long, many of us with ADHD have lived in financial exile—avoiding, hiding, pretending we had it together while feeling completely lost inside. We've internalized messages that we're "bad with money" or "too scattered" or "lacking discipline."

But those messages were never true. They were just **stories told by systems that weren't built for how our brains work.**

What this book gave you is something few financial systems teach:

- **How to stop beating yourself up** and start showing up with compassion

- **How to move forward, even when overwhelmed** by breaking everything into manageable pieces

- **How to see your progress when your brain tells you you're failing** through micro-wins and streak tracking

- **How to rewire your emotional response to mistakes** so setbacks become setups for comebacks

- **How to build trust with yourself again** one small action at a time

- **How to navigate financial crises** without losing your progress or your sanity

- **How to have money conversations** that strengthen rather than damage relationships

- **How to build support systems** that sustain your growth for years to come

This isn't about becoming someone else. It's about becoming **the most authentic version of who you already are**—someone who shows up, resets, and keeps building.

The Science of Small Changes

Let me share something that might surprise you: neuroscience research shows that small, consistent actions create more lasting brain changes than dramatic overhauls.

Every time you completed a 5-minute reset, you weren't just managing money. You were literally **rewiring your neural pathways**. You were teaching your brain that:

- Financial engagement can feel safe

- Progress doesn't require perfection

- You are someone who follows through

- Mistakes don't define you—responses do

Those new neural pathways? They're permanent. They're yours to keep. And they'll serve you not just with money, but in every area of life where you've felt "behind" or "broken."

This is why the reset approach works when willpower fails. **Willpower is a muscle that gets tired. But identity is a story that sustains itself.**

What You've Actually Accomplished

Take a moment to recognize what you've really done here. If you've implemented even a few of the resets in this book, you've:

Reclaimed Your Agency

- You've proven you can open avoided accounts

- You've canceled subscriptions that were draining you

- You've moved money with intention

- You've tracked transactions that used to disappear

Rebuilt Your Self-Trust

- You've shown up on days when you didn't feel like it

- You've reset after mistakes instead of disappearing

- You've celebrated small wins that nobody else sees

- You've spoken to yourself with kindness instead of criticism

Rewired Your Nervous System

- You've taught your brain that money conversations can be calm

- You've created safety around financial engagement

- You've built evidence that you're reliable and capable

- You've developed the muscle of return

These aren't small accomplishments. **These are fundamental life skills** that many people—neurotypical or not—never develop.

Permission to Keep Growing

This isn't about perfection. It's about permission.

Permission to:

- Log in after avoiding your account for a month without self-punishment

- Move $5 when you used to move $0 and call it a win

- Celebrate progress even if it feels tiny compared to where you want to be

- Reset after a mistake instead of disappearing into shame

- Start again—over and over—until the reset becomes your natural rhythm

You have permission to be **exactly where you are** while still moving toward where you want to be.

You have permission to have ADHD and still be financially successful—just not in the ways traditional advice assumes.

You have permission to **define success for yourself** based on your own growth, not someone else's timeline.

What Happens Now

I wish I could tell you that finishing this book means you'll never struggle with money again. That would be a lie, and you deserve better than lies.

You may finish this book and still forget to log into your bank account next week. You might impulse spend during a stressful period. You might ghost your dashboard for a few days. You might mess up in ways that feel familiar and frustrating.

And when that happens—not if, when—come back here.

Reread your favorite chapter. Maybe it's Chapter 2 on what resets really mean. Maybe it's Chapter 13 on breaking shame loops. Maybe it's Chapter 16 on your new identity. Find the one that speaks to where you are right now.

Pick one micro-action. Not ten. Not a complete overhaul. Just one small thing that moves you back into connection with your finances.

Say your reset mantra. The one you created in Chapter 16. Speak it out loud until you feel it in your body, not just your head.

And remember: You don't reset because you failed. You reset because you're **building something that lasts**. And that kind of growth? It compounds. It sticks. It transforms you from the inside out.

The Ripple Effect

Here's something I didn't expect when I started my own reset journey: **the changes rippled far beyond money.**

When you prove to yourself that you can show up for your finances with consistency and compassion, something shifts in how you approach everything else. Relationships. Work. Health. Dreams you've been avoiding.

The person who can reset their money shame is the same person who can reset their dating life after a breakup. The person who can track one transaction daily is the same person who can stick to a workout routine. The person who can break the ADHD financial shame loop is the same person who can **break any pattern that's been keeping them stuck**.

You've been building more than financial skills. **You've been building a new operating system** for your entire life.

Your New Story

Remember the old story? The one that said you were "bad with money" or "too scattered" or "lacking discipline"?

That story is over. Not because you never make mistakes, but because **mistakes no longer define you**.

Your new story goes something like this:

"I'm someone who shows up. I'm someone who resets. I'm someone who moves forward, even from difficult places. I'm someone who treats myself with compassion while still taking action. I'm someone who

doesn't disappear when things get hard—I return, I rebuild, and I keep growing."

That story? It's not aspirational. **It's already true.** Every reset you've done has been evidence of this new identity taking root.

The Community You're Joining

By reading this book and implementing these resets, you're joining a community of people who understand something important: **Success isn't about being perfect. It's about being persistent.**

You're part of a group that knows the difference between self-discipline and self-compassion. That celebrates small wins. That understands the power of starting again.

Somewhere, someone else is opening their avoided account for the first time in weeks. Someone else is canceling a subscription they forgot about. Someone else is moving $5 to savings and feeling proud. Someone else is breaking their own shame loop and choosing to return instead of hide.

You're not alone in this. You never were.

One Last Reset

Right now, as you prepare to close this book, I want you to do one final reset with me.

Take 60 seconds and ask yourself: *"What's one small action I can take today that connects me to the future I'm building?"*

It might be:

- Opening your banking app and taking one breath

- Moving $1 to savings

- Texting a friend about a financial win

- Writing your new money identity statement on a sticky note

- Canceling one subscription

- Simply saying out loud: "I'm someone who resets"

Whatever it is, do it now. Before you move on to the next thing. Before you close this book.

Because that action—however small—is **proof that you're not the same person who started reading**. You're someone who finishes what they start. Someone who takes action. Someone who resets.

Do it now. I'll wait.

...

How did that feel? That small shift in your body, that quiet satisfaction of follow-through? That's the feeling of **alignment between who you are and who you're becoming**.

That feeling is available to you every single day, with every single reset.

The Real Promise

I made you a promise at the beginning of this book. I promised this wasn't about becoming perfect with money. I promised it was about becoming **present with money**.

Have I kept that promise?

You now have:

- A way back into your finances when you've been avoiding them

- Tools that work with your ADHD brain instead of against it

- A shame-free approach to financial mistakes and setbacks

- Micro-actions that build massive identity shifts over time

- Permission to start exactly where you are

But more than that, you have **proof of your own capability**. Every reset you've done is evidence that you're someone who shows up, even when it's hard.

You're Not Starting from Scratch

As you go forward, remember this: **You're not starting from scratch. You're starting from experience.**

You're starting with a reset in your pocket and the proof that you can begin again, every time you need to.

You're starting with tools that work and a story that serves you.

You're starting with the knowledge that **your ADHD brain isn't a liability in your financial life—it's an asset**, when you have the right systems and the right mindset.

Most importantly, you're starting with the **unshakeable truth** that you're someone who doesn't stay stuck. You're someone who resets, rebuilds, and keeps moving forward.

That's not who you're trying to become. **That's who you already are.**

The numbers in your bank account will fluctuate. Your motivation will ebb and flow. Your circumstances will change.

But your identity as someone who resets? **That's yours to keep.**

Use it well. Trust it deeply. And remember:

You don't need a 12-week plan. You don't need to feel ready. You don't need permission from anyone else.

You just need the next five minutes.

And you've already proven you can handle those.

Welcome to your new relationship with money.

Welcome to your new story.

"You don't have to master money overnight. You just have to stop running from it."

—Scott Allan

About Scott Allan

SCOTT ALLAN is an international bestselling author of 40+ books published in 16 languages in the area of personal growth and self-development. He is the author of *Fail Big*, *Undefeated,* and *Do the Hard Things First*.

As a former corporate business trainer in Japan, and **Transformational Mindset Strategist**, Scott has invested over 10,000 hours of research and instructional coaching into the areas of self-mastery and leadership training.

With an unrelenting passion for teaching, building critical life skills, and inspiring people around the world to take charge of their lives, Scott Allan is committed to a path of **constant and never-ending self-improvement**.

You can connect with Scott at:

- www.scottallanbooks.com
- Join Scott Allan's Newsletter

Also Available in the Series

A 5-Step Reset Built for ADHD Brains to Beat
Procrastination, Stop Overthinking, and Stack
Small Wins—One Micro Task at a Time

THE
5 MINUTE
PROCRASTINATION
RESET

SCOTT ALLAN
FROM THE CREATOR OF DO THE HARD THINGS FIRST®